D1356270

THE SHOW MUST GO ON

THE SHOW MUST GO ON

On tour with the LSO in 1912 and 2012

Gareth Davies

Frontispiece images:
Top: Members of the LSO aboard the liner *Baltic*, 1912.
Bottom: Valery Gergiev conducts the LSO in Japan, 2012.

First published 2013 by
Elliott and Thompson Limited
27 John Street, London WC1N 2BX
www.eandtbooks.com

ISBN: 978-1-90873-980-3

Cover design: kid-ethic.com

Typesetting: Louis Mackay / www.louismackaydesign.co.uk

Printed and bound in the UK by T. J. International Ltd., Padstow.

Contents

For Mum and Dad.
For giving me words and music

Introduction

Every musician I know has a tale to tell of life on the road. As in any oral tradition, facts become blurred, names confused and words embellished or lost; but every now and again, someone will recount a story full of detail, as clear as when it took place ... because they were there.

There are two parallel histories of the London Symphony Orchestra. The official version begins in 1904 and continues, uninterrupted, to this day. Alongside it runs another version, a secret history of players' memories and experiences – some of which have been shared along the way, others kept hidden from view, and a very few put down on paper.

In 2007 I started writing a blog for the LSO whenever we went on tour. My posts there served as a record of the orchestra's life during our travels around the globe. As the years passed, describing concert after concert became more challenging, and the entries gradually became a record of my own experiences and memories: my history of the orchestra.

The LSO archives hold evidence of many important moments in the orchestra's history, but one event that still captures the imagination and has passed into LSO folklore is the 1912 trip to America (when, the story goes, the players nearly set sail on the *Titanic*). They were the first European orchestra to undertake a journey across the Atlantic, and there must have been so many stories to tell from that trip – all, it was assumed for decades, lost in time.

However, two years ago I had a chance conversation with our archivist Libby Rice which unexpectedly opened a door to the past. The few sketchy details we had about the 1912 tour were mainly press reports and administrative documents – the official version. What we didn't have were the tall tales and memories of

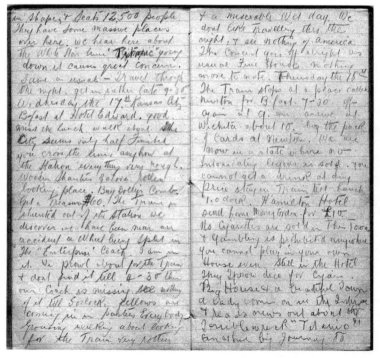

Pages from Charles Turner's 1912 diary, mentioning the *Titanic*.

our musical ancestors, how they felt discovering the New World, what they thought of the concerts, what they ate ... and that, incredibly, was what had suddenly come into Libby's hands. A package had arrived at the LSO office from Roberta Gagliani, who had been clearing out her great-aunt's attic and discovered some of her grandfather's possessions. Among these was a small pocket notebook which mentioned the LSO. Realizing its significance, Roberta sent it to Libby.

The notebook belonged to LSO timpani player Charles Turner, and chronicled his experiences during that 1912 tour to North America. Incredibly, a few weeks later we were contacted by Jack Nisbet, who sent us a copy of a diary written by his grandfather, flautist Henry Nisbet, during the same period.

Overnight, many of the questions I had were answered, gaps in our knowledge filled; through Turner's and Nisbet's words, we had a glimpse into what life was like for them on the road exactly one hundred years ago. Some of the stories that had been presumed lost were sitting on the page in front of me.

Two things struck me as I went through the diaries: how much has changed, and how much remains the same. It was then that the idea for this book entered my head. I had originally intended it to be an extended blog entry, but as my research drew me in and more information came to light and the project got bigger, the parallels between the LSO in 1912 and in 2012 became more pronounced, and I just kept on writing. Each chapter in the book about 1912 is followed by a chapter about 2012. As the story from last century revealed itself, the narrative naturally fell into themes: travel, conductors, discovering new places, being away from home and, finally, dealing with life and death.

The book will introduce you to the players of 1912, and to the musicians I work with every day in 2012; to legendary conductor Arthur Nikisch and to our current principal conductor, the mesmeric Valery Gergiev. We will travel from London to Japan, China, most of Europe and, importantly, New York City, exactly one hundred years after the orchestra's first visit. I hope it gives you a unique insight into what makes an orchestra tick, but also what it's really like to be a musician travelling with one of the world's greatest orchestras. The travel arrangements and working hours have changed, but many things haven't – not least, the kind of individual who decides to become an orchestral musician. This is the story of the London Symphony Orchestra in the words of the players themselves: three musicians, one orchestra, a century apart.

I Upbeat Before the Downbeat
1912

It's 1.30 p.m. on Thursday 28th March, 1912. Euston Station is unusually crowded as the one hundred musicians of the London Symphony Orchestra stand around saying their goodbyes to friends and family before embarking on a historic tour to the United States of America.

No European orchestra has ever travelled across the Atlantic before, and this departure is the beginning of an adventure that has been two years in the planning. The newspapers in London and New York have been full of articles publicizing the tour, pictures of the conductor Arthur Nikisch have been plastered on the front page of the *New York Times*, and gossip columns have whispered about his alleged fee of $1,000 a night. The headline in an article published in New York on that day boldly describes the tour as 'An American Conquest' and even the King himself has given it his seal of approval. For a fledgling orchestra, born out of rebellion only eight years earlier, it is an early statement of intent that the LSO is forging

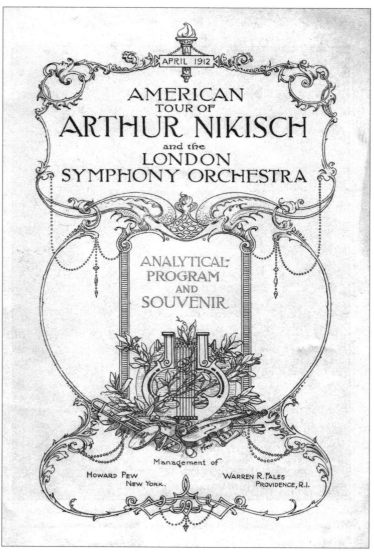

Souvenir programme from the 1912 American tour.

its own path; it is a young, ambitious newcomer. Sit down, be quiet, and listen.

Sir Thomas Beecham had planned to take the Queen's Hall Orchestra to America a few years before – plans that came to nothing – and perhaps it was his failure that galvanized the board of directors at the time to make sure the LSO made the first move. However, the name of the London Symphony Orchestra on its own was not enough. In the last few months before commercial recording of the symphonic repertoire really took off, only people who had travelled had heard the legendary ensembles of central Europe, and the mythology of these great performers loomed large in people's minds. The Berlin Philharmonic, Leipzig Gewandhaus and America's own Boston Symphony Orchestra were the Holy Grail for an orchestral enthusiast. However, surely this dynamic ensemble with an already turbulent history was going to be welcomed in the land of the free.

From his offices on 42nd Street, the New York-based promoter Howard Pew had been bringing musical acts of varying sorts to American audiences since 1885. He had had great success persuading Presidents Harrison and McKinley to allow him to take the US Marine Band around the country, as well as bringing a host of Italian opera stars to sing for the eager American public. A long-held dream of his was to bring a premier European ensemble across. Nobody had done it before, and he was a man with a shrewd business sense as well as high artistic standards, so the LSO was not his first point of call in 1910. He knew that to sell tickets and encourage other rich benefactors to help him make it happen he needed a big name on the rostrum; and so, before he could decide on an ensemble, the first piece of the jigsaw was to secure the services of the conductor Arthur Nikisch.

Nikisch was revered in America, thanks to his highly successful tenure as principal conductor with the Boston Symphony

Orchestra. His performances were still being talked about 19 years later, especially as he hadn't returned to the USA; audiences were desperate to see him again. Before the advent of the jet-setting conductor, audiences had to wait a long time between appearances, which only increased the mystique surrounding Nikisch and consequently his draw at the box office. The combination of high artistic standards and box office receipts was what attracted Pew.

From the outset, Nikisch made it clear that he was interested in coming on one condition: that he could bring the orchestra of his choice. Knowing that it would always be the conductor rather than the orchestra that would sell tickets, and also aware that Nikisch would hardly agree to come all the way back to the States with a second-rate band, Pew agreed immediately. Nikisch then proudly announced that the only orchestra he would consider accompanying across the Atlantic was the London Symphony Orchestra.

Pew must have been delighted. He knew that bringing Nikisch back for a triumphant return was going to generate huge press interest. It would also attract some of the musically-minded philanthropists he had in mind to help pay for the small matter of bringing an entire orchestra and their instruments across the sea, not to mention insuring their instruments and paying for food, hotels, travel, and music hire. The costs were going to be high, the risks even higher; everything had to be right for the tour to be a success. However, as Henry Kniebel wrote in the *New York Tribune* in 1912 shortly before the tour began:

> In the highest form of instrumental art, as in the hybrid form of opera which chiefly lives on in affectation and fad, it is the singer and not the song that challenges attention from the multitude. We used to have prima donnas in New York whose names on a program ensured financial success for the performance ...

for prima donna ... read conductor, and a parallel is established
in orchestral art which is even more humiliating than that per-
vading our opera house.

Kniebel's disapproving remarks suggested a future in which
a new world of superstar conductors travelled the globe, com-
manding adoration and large fees: exactly what Pew wanted.
Negotiations began.

As plans progressed for the 1912 tour, LSO managing director
Thomas Busby realized that if it was to become a reality, financial support would be needed – preferably from both sides of
the Atlantic. Howard Pew was constantly sending letters to the
board of the LSO about ways to keep down costs, which were
beginning to spiral out of control owing to the sheer scale of the
tour. At a meeting, the orchestra had agreed to the trip and sent a
list of requirements to Pew. He was to provide

All meals, three a day and accommodation in which not more
than two should occupy a room. Mr Pew should provide a capable baggage and instrument porter in addition to the LSO
porter and that $20,000 to be deposited with Brown and Shipley
and Co. prior to the departure from England.

Ultimately, most of these demands were met, but in a more creative way than perhaps the board had imagined. Accommodation
was indeed provided, a hotel in New York being the first port of
call; although, as Charles Turner reveals in his 1912 diary, this
was not quite what they were expecting: 'Go to Hotel Victoria,
Broadway. A giant place but more trouble. They have put 3 or 4
beds in one room. Large, beautiful rooms but the fellows don't
like it. Beautiful lunch anyhow at 12 o'clock.'

The player-to-room ratio was not as per the contract
(although a stationary hotel was a temporary measure in any
case), but at least Turner's lunch was satisfactory. After leaving

New York on April 9th, the players would not sleep in a hotel room again until the end of their trip, on April 28th. To save costs whilst still keeping his end of the agreement, Howard Pew had come up with the idea of sending the orchestra around America on a specially chartered train. The fly in the ointment was that the players' accommodation during the trip would consist solely of several shared sleeping cars on the train. Turner's diary reveals that immediately after most concerts the band would trudge back to their train, drink, smoke, and play cards until the early morning, and then catch a little sleep in their bunks. This was not the accommodation they might have hoped for, but then, as now, in the arts world, every penny counted.

At a board meeting in November 1911, Thomas Busby had presented a piece of paper that would be of great help in securing funding for the tour. He had come directly from a meeting at Buckingham Palace, where he had asked the King to consider giving his patronage to the LSO, pointing out that this would greatly benefit the special relationship between Britain and America. There was an ulterior motive to his request, in that 18 members of the LSO were also members of the King's Private Band, and as such were contracted to be available to perform at the palace at all times. Many were key players, and so by gaining the King's patronage, Busby ensured that these players would be released to play in the concert tour. There was one small condition: all 18 members were required to wear three King's Medals at every engagement in America, so that members of the public could pick them out from the rest of the orchestra. Busby and Pew must have been delighted; the letter from the King was proudly displayed at the front of the souvenir programme.

In one of the many pre-tour articles that appeared in the American press, Busby, when asked about the repertoire for the tour, declined to reveal it, but boasted that the audience was in for a treat and a surprise. The truth was that there were huge arguments going on between Pew and the LSO board about what should be played, and who should pay for it. Busby therefore had no clear idea of the intended programme.

In a 1911 board meeting, a letter from Pew was read out in which he complained that he 'didn't see why he should share in the royalty charged for the Richard Strauss works'. One reason why the LSO thought that he should pay was that he had requested that they play Strauss in the first place. The board had come up with a series of programmes that was at first rejected on the basis that, with so much travelling, it would be better to concentrate on two or three programmes and repeat them around the country, thereby saving on rehearsal time and costs. At this time, the orchestra was associated with the music of Sir Edward Elgar, and the board was keen to programme some of his works; however, Howard Pew's representative in London – a Mr Blumenburg – made his feelings clear on the matter at a meeting in July 1911:

> Mr Blumenburg was dissatisfied with the programme as arranged and [said] that more Brahms, Strauss, Mozart and Bach music should be included and that if any Elgar items were included he would fire the whole scheme up as far as he was concerned.

Busby was asked at the same meeting to draw up some new programmes fairly swiftly, with no Elgar.

Once the patronage of the King had been secured, funding and sponsorship from sources on both sides of the Atlantic followed. Towards the end of 1911, the musical instrument manufacturers Boosey and Hawkes offered to donate trumpets, horns, and trombones to the orchestra with the proviso that the players actually played on them throughout the tour, which seemed a reasonable request. A financial compromise was made that

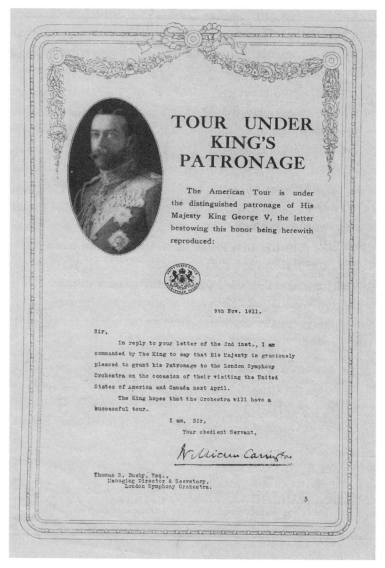

The letter from Buckingham Palace confirming the King's patronage.

required the musicians themselves to insure their own instru-ments, something that Busby boasted in the *New York Times* made the value of $500,000 the 'most valuable set of instruments ever to make the journey across by boat'. No publicity opportu-nity was missed. Finally, Howard Pew managed to secure a pri-vate donor whose patronage and substantial investment would make the whole trip possible, in the form of one Warren Fales.

Warren R. Fales of Providence, Rhode Island, was well known across the country as a patron of good music. He claimed to own the biggest manufacturing plant in the world, making machin-ery for the cotton mills. As a result, he was very wealthy indeed, and spent a lot of his free time and money on the arts. He was conductor of the American Brass Band of Providence, which was a famous ensemble at the time and claimed to have the 'most notable bass drum in the USA'. Very well travelled in Europe, he even boasted of having made a complete circuit of the globe several times.

One thing is certain. The LSO would not have been able to make the trip if it hadn't been for the financial help Fales provid-ed. Howard Pew had the ideas; Fales the money to realize them.

2 International Commuters

2012

Super Mario goes to Sonic City

After our first concert in Osaka, we all piled onto a bullet train, which is always one of the highlights of touring Japan. Unlike the trains on which I am normally incarcerated, these ones are fast and clean, leave on time, and look cool. The efficiency with which everything runs in Japan extends to the railways, and to keep to their tight schedule there is a time limit for the opening of the doors. When you get on or off a bullet train there's a sort of high-pitched electronic whistle, and a very twitchy guard stands and waves a torch down the platform to signal that it's time to shut the doors and move off. There is a guard on every door, whereas in Britain we have one guard for every train – strikes, leaves, and weather permitting.

You can imagine that for a two-week tour of the London Symphony Orchestra, suitcases are on the large side. So that we don't bring the Japanese transport system to its knees, our cases are transported for us on a separate truck, leaving us relatively unencumbered and ready for the frantic race that is disembarking. On the first day we arrived it was chucking it down with rain, prompting many of us to buy cheap umbrellas. The only ones we could easily find were old-fashioned long umbrellas, the kind British businessmen used to swing briskly on their way to work in the days when everyone dressed as an extra from *Mary Poppins*. Because of this, we were a large group of Westerners all looking terribly English indeed. All we needed was a copy of the *Financial Times* under our arms and the cliché would have been complete.

The train pulled into the station, with most of the orchestra poised to get off as quickly as possible. The doors opened and we jumped off one by one, opening our automatic umbrellas with a *click, whump* sound. The scene was reminiscent of a parachute regiment being flung out of a plane. We leapt onto the platform as the guard was gradually becoming frantic: his door was obviously going to be the last to give the green light in the chain of command. All the other guards along the platform were giving him evil looks. He started to sweat and shout. This would normally have been the point at which Sue Mallet, our director of planning, joined in with the shouting until the guard was shocked into submission. However, she was in London, and this tour was being run by Mario de Sa, our tour manager and one of the coolest customers there is. He often greeted us in the morning with a cheery 'Morning, chaps!' I expect in a former life he was a pipe-smoking World War II fighter pilot and a thoroughly good egg.

Mario remained calm under the increasing pressure being exerted by the guard. The high-pitched whistling was replaced with a lower beeping noise, sending the guard into a silent rage; perhaps we were affecting his targets for the week. Realizing that the doors were soon to shut, Mario raised his long umbrella and, without taking his eyes off the guard, smilingly jammed the end of it into the door's way, preventing it from closing. It began beeping more loudly. The last of the jumpers appeared on the platform, and Mario leaned forward and looked into the carriage, which was empty apart from a shocked-looking elderly couple wondering what had happened to their normally prompt and reliable train service. Just as the guard spotted the umbrella jammed in the door, Mario removed it with another smile and said, 'Thank you very much.' The door closed, relieved, and the train moved off one minute late. Mario ran to the front of the group, holding his umbrella up. 'This way, chaps!'

We were in Omiya, at the fantastically named Sonic City, to play Mussorgsky/Ravel, *Pictures at an Exhibition*. I hate this piece. I don't really know why. Maybe it's because I've played it in so many education concerts in my time, or outdoors in fields. I often

Nigel Thomas (timpani) and Sharon Williams (piccolo) get some rest on a train somewhere in Japan.

find it a bitty piece – lots of disjointed pictures – and it's tricky to play. I should have seen it coming, of course: Valery Gergiev, our principal conductor, started pulling it to pieces in the rehearsal just before the concert. He wanted more extremes of dynamics and sound, more theatre, more effort in general.

As Phil Cobb, our principal trumpet, threw the opening volley out into the hall, the majestic sound of the LSO brass filled the room, but there was no pause between pictures for Valery as he plunged straight into the low, aggressive burble of 'Gnomus'. I saw a lady in the front row jump in her seat. Valery has the ability to pluck details from the music that no one else seems to pick up on; almost as if he has access to a different score from everyone else. He takes well-known pieces and breathes new life into them. The pauses in this movement were long and ominous before Lorenzo Iosco's sinuous bass clarinet gurgled around the bass section. But it was 'Baba Yaga' that took my breath away.

I have become used to playing 'Baba Yaga' in Discovery concerts for eight-year-olds at which, during the pause bars, a presenter on stage talks, describing the terrifying image of a hut on chicken's legs going round eating kids. They always seem to conclude by saying, '… and he swallowed the children: yum, yum.' I suppose we don't want to send the kids home scared, but this has spoiled the piece somewhat for me. Until, that is, Valery launched into the most awesome, abrasive version I have ever heard. There was no need for talking: the full might of the orchestra screamed from the stage and grabbed people from their seats, rendering 'Baba Yaga' truly nightmare-inducing. As we finally reached the 'Great Gate of Kiev', the whole orchestra was in full flight, and it was over all too quickly.

On the train back, we boarded in record time, and Super Mario relaxed as we left Sonic City behind. I sat down next to my friend Chi-Yu Mo, a clarinet player.

'I normally hate that piece.'

'Me too.'

'It was awesome.'

'Yum, yum.'

Quite.

The long haul

On my suburban train last week, I read in the *Metro* free news-paper an extraordinarily in-depth article claiming that if you spend two hours of each working day commuting, by the end of your working life you will have spent twelve years of your life sitting on a train. Or, in my case, standing up.

It struck me that as LSO players, we often spend significantly more time than this 'commuting' to various places around the globe. This week, for instance, we are spending more than 24 hours in transit. This is not unusual for us, but does mean that if you spend your entire working life with the orchestra (I joined when I was 28, and am now older), you will spend something like 20 years commuting.

It is a measure of what an odd existence life in an orchestra can be. We are currently on the second day of a trip to Spain and Portugal. Yesterday I got up at 5.30 a.m. and drove to Stansted Airport, caught a flight to Valencia, had a bite to eat, then went to a rehearsal and concert. I crawled into bed at about 1 a.m. We played Schubert 5 and Bruckner 7; or was it Bruckner 5 and Schubert 7? I forget ...

The hall in Valencia is one of my favourites: it has a very good sound, and you are surrounded by the audience. It almost feels like playing in the round, which can be unnerving if something goes wrong. However, with Sir Colin Davis wielding the baton we are in very safe hands. I love playing Bruckner 7 with him.

In such a huge work, you really need a conductor who understands the overall architecture of the piece, otherwise it can end up sounding like a long line of unrelated chunks of sound. Sir Colin keeps the music flowing, and doesn't let the long melodies wallow around. When we do slow down at an important climax – such as where the cymbals and triangle make their only appearance, in the slow movement – it makes a huge impact. By the end of the symphony I always have a sense of the long, arching journey we have made from start to finish. Last night's audience certainly agreed, as Sir Colin was called back on four times.

Tonight in Lisbon we are performing Schubert's Unfinished Symphony and Bruckner 6. (Interesting that Bruckner's 9th was unfinished, but is never called 'the unfinished'. I suspect this may be because, even in this state, it is over an hour long. Bruckner's 'thank goodness it's unfinished' symphony, maybe?) I shall leave you with a mathematical observation.

The *Metro* piece suggests that you spend twelve years of your life commuting if you travel two hours a day. Sir Colin Davis is 80, and probably travels many more miles than the average commuter. As his working life is already far longer than most normal men, by my calculations, he will soon have 'commuted' for almost 120 years.

This either means my maths isn't what it used to be, or – just maybe – the newspaper article has some slightly inaccurate figures. I know: it shocked me, too.

The Italian job

London's black cabs have rescued me from certain lateness on many occasions. As someone who usually walks or rides a Brompton bike, it's only when things are desperate that I get into a cab. It gives me a feeling of self-importance to jump in the back and say 'Barbican Centre, please, and don't spare the horses!' I wonder whether anyone ever asks cab drivers to take the scenic route?

As you probably know, black-cab drivers have to pass an exam for which they must memorize all the street names in the city and be able to navigate them successfully. This is called 'The Knowledge'. It is astonishing how much information they manage to retain about the muddled street system, while still leaving room for unique opinions on important world matters, usually involving Boris Johnson, the cost of the Olympics in 2012, and the dregs of society (otherwise known as cyclists). Sort-of-joking aside, it's easy to take for granted the good things on your own doorstep. As I type this, my knuckles are still white with fear after gripping my seat very tightly indeed during a taxi ride in Turin.

On Friday we arrived in Pisa to kick off this Italian tour, and what a beautiful place it is. The famous tower seems to lean much more than pictures suggest, and the surrounding buildings are breathtaking in their beauty. It was hot in the Duomo for the concert, and guest leader Andrew Haveron's *Lark Ascending* soared beautifully around the wooden ceiling, enjoying some much-missed summer warmth. Yesterday, a Saturday, we were greeted with a train strike and had to endure a very long coach journey to Milan, where the audience was appreciative. Playing Mozart and Beethoven with Sir Colin conducting continues to be one of my greatest pleasures in the LSO; he makes it so much fun.

After the concert we took buses to our hotel in Turin, arriving at about 2.30 a.m. A very long day indeed. The hotel is a huge building that used to be the Fiat factory. If you've seen the film *The Italian Job* – the original one with Michael Caine, set in Italy, not the American remake – it features heavily. There is a famous scene in which three Minis are driven through the factory and up onto the rooftop test track. This really did exist and, I suppose, honed the drivers' skills somewhat, as it is a very long way down if you skid off. These days it is the hotel jogging track, complete with banked corners. I went up there this morning and there were two blokes running round making car revving noises. As well as the race-track scene, you may recall the fantastic stunt driving through the streets, pavements, and shopping arcades of Turin, where the Minis are driven down steps and through shops at breakneck speed. I can't help thinking that whilst London cab drivers spend a couple of years going around London on a moped with an *A–Z* learning their craft, the cab driver I had last night simply watched the *Italian Job* driving sequences and was promptly handed his keys. I'm not sure whether he did actually mount the pavement, as everything was too blurred. When he heard my accent he locked the doors, looked at me in the rear-view mirror, started whistling 'The Self-Preservation Society', and took off. It was truly terrifying.

We have a concert this evening in the hall inside the factory building: a fantastic hall, with a very reverberant acoustic. I listened to the rehearsal of Vaughan Williams's Symphony No. 4, as I don't play in the piece. The hall allows the quiet passages to float effortlessly towards the back, and the loud moments rock the foundations. It should be a great evening: a great hall, great music, and I can't think of a better conductor to lead us in this repertoire.

♩ ♩ ♩

As the orchestra attacked the final *forte* chord of the symphony, Colin raised his eyebrows and looked taken aback at the sheer level of sound. He turned to the auditorium, seemingly watching the sound echo around the hall, then turned back to the orchestra and said something that made them all laugh. I couldn't hear it from where I was sitting, but I have a sneaking suspicion it was 'You were only supposed to blow the bloody doors off!'

Far, far, far, far East

I think someone has moved Japan since I was last here.

It's taken us such a long time to get here, it's the only explanation I can come up with. I left home at midday on Monday, and finally got into bed in Sapporo at midnight on Wednesday. Even taking into account that Japan is nine hours ahead of London, that's one hell of a long time: about 28 hours of travelling. For those of you who travel business class and sit on twelve-hour flights there: well, if you carry on walking for another 50 metres, you'll reach cattle class, where all of us sit. Evidently the music business doesn't qualify. It's a bit cramped, to be honest, and even someone as short as me finds it a squeeze for that long. On this occasion we arrived at Osaka airport, where the efficiency of the staff meant that (unlike at Heathrow) we were through immigration and baggage in about 20 minutes. Unfortunately we then had to wait another six hours for our flight to Sapporo.

I have never been so bored in my life. It was Chi's birthday, but no matter how many times we wished him many happy returns, no matter how many free drinks he was given, no matter how many cards he received, we couldn't get away from the fact that today, his birthday, was rubbish. To make matters worse, the orchestra had been split into two groups, and the other group left London after us and arrived in Sapporo before us. There was a secret ballot, so I'm told – so secret, in fact, that nobody knows who did it. Maybe I should start being nice to Sue Mallet again.

Rehearsal in Japan.

When we finally arrived at Sapporo airport, we faced an hour-and-a-half bus journey to the hotel. I could resist sleep no longer, and finally drifted off. When we pulled up outside the hotel I could see the other half of the orchestra in the bar opposite, eating and drinking and trying really hard not to look smug. They were totally unsuccessful. I piled straight in for some food and beer until I lost the ability to talk, which made some people very happy, then collapsed into bed and slept heavily.

We had a free day on Wednesday, and went to a volcano. It hasn't erupted for a while (and didn't when we went), but it was free to get in, so I didn't complain. It was very nice to walk around after being stuck on public transport for a few days. Once again, I slept well last night, unusually for me in Japan.

Today we started the musical part of our tour. At the rehearsal, the band and Valery sounded and looked a little sleepy. He asked us to save our energy for the concert, which we did. The people I work with never cease to amaze me: we all got changed, Gergiev walked on stage, and the orchestra played as if its life depended on it. I was only in Prokofiev's *Romeo and Juliet* in the second half, but the audience demanded an encore. We played the March from *The Love for Three Oranges*, an excellent encore, loud and short! Tomorrow the tour starts in earnest. We leave early and go hell for leather for the next week, with a concert every day. We have to fly from the North Island to the South Island. Let's hope they haven't moved that, too.

This way, this way, that way, this way, this way or that way ...

I am writing this whilst travelling unbelievably smoothly and quickly on the Shinkansen train to Tokyo. You probably know it best as the bullet train, and it certainly lives up to its name. Its aerodynamically shaped front end looks like the love child of a train, a space shuttle, and a mutant duck, and when it shoots through the station at full speed the sense of harnessed power is awesome.

Today, we are on the 9.26 train. The carriages are double deckers, and we are on the lower deck, so the eye level from our seats is level with the platform, giving me a great vantage point from which to study Japanese footwear. The train is clean, all the toilets work, and the staff are polite. As we pull out of the station we accelerate at incredible speed, and everything becomes a blur apart from the mountain ranges and Mount Fuji in the distance.

This is my sixth visit to Japan. Every time I come, I am astonished by the efficiency with which it is run: the trains are on time, everything is clean, and the concert halls – even in out-of-the-way places – are spectacular. When I was lost at the station earlier in the week a young lady from the railway company asked me in perfect English if I needed help, and then proceeded to help me buy the correct ticket, take me to the platform, and make sure I was sitting in the right seat. As someone accustomed to the begrudging, monosyllabic grunting that passes for customer service in Britain, I was quite astonished.

The people who shepherd us round Japan are from the Kajimoto concert management company. If they were allowed to run countries, I am convinced they would end world hunger in a flash (although they would probably be more precise than me, and end it on a Monday at 9.23 a.m. GMT). From the moment we arrived, greeted by a smiling face and an LSO sign pointing us in the right direction, we have been looked after like royalty. In Sapporo earlier this week, we actually had to walk from the hotel to the concert hall unaided – but to prevent us getting lost on the way, one of our guides sat in the hotel foyer and showed us which door to go out of (there are two doors, you see). I walked a few yards to the edge of the hotel grounds and found an LSO logo on the lamppost with an arrow pointing left. I turned left. As I did so, I could see the next LSO sign on the next lamppost: it pointed straight on. I went straight on. When I reached this sign I began to panic – it was a pedestrian crossing which I had to negotiate on my own – but, fortunately, I could see another LSO logo across the road. I crossed. This next sign had the logo, and two arrows, one pointing left and the other pointing straight ahead but saying 'slippery way'. Faced with this sudden test of initiative, I decided to live dangerously and go the slippery way. It was indeed slippery. At the end of this road was – you get the idea – a sign with the logo, telling me to turn left. I could see the hall now. When I reached the stage door there was another sign telling me to go in, and even more signs inside showed me where the dressing rooms, stage, and toilets were. By the time I had finished my walk to the hall, my eyes were exhausted.

The journey took three minutes.

Earlier this week, one of my friends left his mobile phone on a train seat. Back home, you would have simply cancelled the number and replaced the handset, as the chances of it being recovered were slim. On our return journey we went to the information office and filled in a form, not really certain that it was the right one. It took us an hour to get back to the hotel, and on our return there was a message at reception. The lost phone had been picked up, handed in, and would be delivered to the hotel at 10.30 the following morning unless we needed it earlier, in which case they could bring it over straight away. I expect they'd topped up his credit too.

When we arrived at our hotel yesterday another of our tour managers, Miriam Loeben, was presented with a letter from the previous hotel which consisted of a list of items accidentally left behind by members of the orchestra. The summary gives an idea of the attention to detail that's typical of this country.

Left Articles in LSO Rooms

One jacket

Five coins

One Eurostar ticket (used)

One paper cup

One cleaning cloth

One nightgown from unknown room, cleared up with sheets by mistake

What a brilliant place this is!

Ich bin ein Frankfurter

Yet again, I am sitting on a train, this time somewhere in Germany. I seem to spend a disproportionate amount of my time writing on trains. When we reached the Essen Hauptbahnhof this morning it was snowing heavily but, much to my surprise, the locals carried on as normal. There was already grit on the platform, which makes me think that they knew in advance that it was going to snow: clever chaps, these Germans. The train on the opposite platform arrived on time, and it was at this point that someone shouted that we were in fact on the wrong platform. All eighty or so of us rushed down the not-slippery ramps and made a desperate dash for the Frankfurt train.

We managed to get on in time, providing some rush-hour amusement for the Essen commuters. I held my breath, though, in anticipation of the situation I felt sure would ensue; after all the silly British people ran to get on the train, it would of course be cancelled due to EXTREME WEATHER CONDITIONS. Imagine my astonishment when the train pulled smoothly away with absolutely no traction problems whatsoever. This was doubly impressive given that, before the train had arrived, I had clearly seen some leaves on the line. I had thought that this was the sort of thing that happened only in Japan, but it seems German efficiency is also second to none. It must have something to do with that famous German proverb, *Vorsprung durch Technik*. Roughly translated, it means 'You call that snow? You should see Mannheim in January.'

Last night's concert went well. The hall in Essen is nice, but it's one of those places where they leave the house lights on and we stare at you and you stare at us. I thought that the audience looked bored all the way through. It made me try and play even better, but they still looked bored. However, as soon as we finished Beethoven 5, they all cheered and stood up to applaud. I'd mistaken the intense concentration on their faces for boredom – they loved it.

The hall in Frankfurt is one of my favourites, with a grandeur that makes every concert feel like a real event. Its ornate foyers have big, sweeping staircases and velvet curtains that exude Continental glamour. Backstage there is a café for performers, which used to have one of the most terrifying women in Germany serving. She could communicate only by shouting, and unless I was very hungry, I used the chocolate machine in the corner; it was more sympathetic.

As we finished the final rehearsal of the tour, ushers shooed us off the stage, keen to open the doors and let the audience in. We trundled off to the relative calm of the dressing rooms, away from the stage-sweepers and the café lady, to get changed. Every once in a while, a loud voice came over the speakers to let us know how many minutes of freedom remained before the concert:

'Ladies and gentlemen of ze orchestra, it is now 19.15.'

The concert was to start at 8 p.m., so I had plenty of time to get changed and buy some chocolate. A short while and one cufflink later, another ear-splitting announcement:

'Ladies and gentlemen of ze orchestra, it is now 19.30.'

Most musicians like a bit of peace and quiet before a show. However, with all this efficiency, I was starting to think I might have mistranslated *Vorsprung durch Wassisname*. This was confirmed by the hoots of laughter at the final announcement before we went on stage.

'Ladies and Gentlemen of ze orchestra, it is now 19.45.'

The men in the band room cheered.

For us, the tour was over.

The Esraehtniniap* volcano thingy

People often ask me whether it is stressful being in the LSO. The answer is not simple. Let's take this week, for example (already, I can tell you that there is no such thing as a typical week at LSO Towers). As I write this we are once again on a train, making our way from Frankfurt to Hanover and then on to Dortmund before returning to London for concerts on Wednesday and Thursday. The concerts on this trip are all the same programme:

L'Après-midi d'un faune (Debussy)

Symphony in C (Stravinsky) or La Mer (Debussy)

Firebird complete ballet (Stravinsky)

We performed this show in London. We have four concerts on tour, and then we repeat in London on Wednesday.

L'Après-midi is the slowest, longest, most terrifyingly lonely phrase I have to play as an orchestral flautist. The piece is usually placed at the beginning of a concert and starts with a four-bar phrase played by the flute. It requires huge amounts of air, great breath control, nerves of steel, and an excellent dry cleaner. After the first four bars, which are not conducted, everybody else joins in, and gradually one of the most beguiling pieces of music ever written for orchestra unfolds like a flower in the morning. It begins on a C sharp (probably the worst note on the flute) and phrase after phrase of long, controlled playing ends about twelve minutes later, leaving me light-headed from oxygen deprivation.

Playing last night in Frankfurt was interesting, as it's one of the biggest halls we play in. I always worry about controlling the air stream so that the opening phrase is played in the way the composer wishes, but also so that I don't run out of breath

---

* Some names have been changed to protect the privacy of individual volcanoes.

before the end. To do this, you need to control the rate at which you blow. I make no apologies for getting scientific and technical about my mystical art here: before I start, I take a really big breath – I mean huge, so that I'm about to burst – and then I let it out slowly, hopefully running out just after the end of the phrase.

In theory, this is straightforward; but in the reality of a concert, when you are faced with a huge hall and total silence, nerves play their part, and a voice in my head shouts: '*You're not going to make it! You didn't take enough breath!*' The other thing you have to factor in is that conductors sometimes like to conduct the last bar of the solo, and some of them think it's a good idea to slow it down, thereby laying waste to my perfect air management. It's a bit like a Formula One driver having his car filled up with exactly the right amount of fuel to get round Silverstone. He gets to the last lap, he's in the lead with ten miles to go and ten miles' worth of fuel left, and then he turns a corner to find that the local council has implemented traffic-calming measures since his last lap. He stops 300 yards short of the line and feels like a bit of a berk.

In a big hall like Frankfurt, you worry about whether the people at the back will be able to hear you. When I play quietly, I have to blow softly, which helps to get through the phrase. To play more loudly, I have to blow harder (are you still with me? Good), which means I have to take an even bigger breath. (I bet you haven't thought about things like this since you were a kid and tried to see who could stay underwater for the longest without drowning. I always won.)

Now, you may imagine that doing this every night for a week, and recording it for LSO Live and Radio 3 broadcast, was the most stressful thing in my life at the moment. Wrong. It's that erupting volcano in Iceland that's causing travel chaos in Europe. It's making life very difficult for us, and especially for our management team – who are excelling themselves, but, I'm sure, would rather not have to do so. On Saturday we flew uneventfully to Dublin to perform in its marvellous hall, arrived in time for lunch, and spent a lovely sunny afternoon there. As I was getting ready for the rehearsal I noticed those all-too-familiar pictures of the volcano spewing its contents over Europe on the televisions in the hotel foyer. The headlines were all about closing British airspace overnight. I could feel another long weekend on buses coming on. By the time I reached the hall, Miriam and Super Mario had already rearranged the travel arrangements for the next morning, and there were rumours that Sue Mallet had been dispatched to stop the volcano simply by giving it a stern look. We had to get to Frankfurt before they closed Irish airspace; Belfast was already shut. The orchestra was told that we would have to leave on our charter plane two hours earlier than scheduled the next morning to ensure a safe departure. After the show I had a little Guinness (because it's a legal requirement), retired to my room, and set three alarms for 4.30 a.m.

We managed to take off before the ash began to fall over Dublin and arrived at the hotel in Frankfurt, a little weary, as they were putting the breakfast things away. British airspace was closed a few hours later. The trouble is that we are due to fly back to London on Wednesday morning before our concert, and at the moment the volcano is still erupting and the ash cloud is predicted to be over Germany by then.

If the volcano stops, and if the ash cloud doesn't reach Germany, and if British airspace is open ... we are booked to fly with British Airways on the way home. Their cabin crew are due to strike on Wednesday. But fear not: Miriam, Super Mario, and their team are already sorting out Plan C. We in the flute section, of course, have a Plan D: Siobhan Grealy, our second flute player, is off sick this week, so our old friend Martin Parry is with us in her place. He retired a while ago after a long and distinguished career and, as luck would have it, one of his hobbies is flying planes – the kind with propellers, which laugh in the face of ash clouds. We're going to have a whip-round, and if we can get hold of a plane, we'll get the whole flute section back. So one way or another we'll see you at the Barbican, where the flute section will be present and correct. Of course, that means that the first four bars of the concert will be as described above, and we'll busk the rest.

China crisis

To-do list

1. Pack tails – done

2. Pack normal clothes – done

3. Pack flute and piccolo – done

4. Pack laptop and book – done

5. Check tube strike (not until Tuesday)

6. Check no engineering works on train – done

7. Check flight details on Internet for delays – done

8. Pack passport

9. Unpack passport and pack correct passport with Chinese visa

10. Check Blackberry for last-minute-panic phone calls from Sue – done

11. Repack Blackberry (and charger)

12. Check in at Terminal 5 and go through security

13. Relax and wait for flight

14. Leave on time

I am especially careful with my preparations when we go to China, as it isn't always easy to find things there that you have forgotten: an iPhone charger, for instance. Or Marmite.

I sat next to viola player Malcolm Johnston on the flight. Sue and Miriam were looking as relaxed as they can, which is most people's breaking point, and we were chatting to one of the air stewards, who turned out to be an LSO subscriber. The one thing I enjoy about long haul is the in-flight entertainment, so I was taking the opportunity to watch a film I can't watch with my kids. I was five minutes into *Kick-Ass* (highly inappropriate viewing for children) when the screen went blank and the captain made an announcement in the calm, sing-song tone of a golf commentator: 'Ladies and gentlemen, this is the captain speaking. I'm sure you will have noticed that we have turned round, and are heading back to Heathrow. Also, we are jettisoning fuel as a safety precaution. One of the engines has developed a fault, we have shut it down, and we will be landing in about half an hour. Nothing to worry about; it's perfectly normal.'

Normal? I looked out of the window, and saw a jet of aviation fuel streaming out of the wing like a fireman's hose. I looked at the map on the screen, to check that the fuel was going into the sea, and noticed that we were fast approaching Kent. I had a dreadful image of some poor bloke in a pub in Maidstone going outside for a quick fag, lighting up, and spontaneously combusting.

The LSO-friendly steward came and spoke to me, as he was concerned we wouldn't get to the show on time. That was not my main concern at that moment, but I suggested he go and speak to Sue. 'She is sitting four rows in front of me, with steam coming out of her ears,' I told him.

To be honest, if they hadn't told us there was a problem, I would never have known. We landed, trooped back to the terminal, and waited.

I may have had a beer.

As the orchestra had flown back from Germany only the day before, this was an unwelcome setback to the journey, but these things happen. It made a change from a volcano, I suppose. In the event, we were meant to arrive in Shanghai at 8 a.m. on Monday, but finally landed at about 1.30 p.m. A bus to the hotel got me to my room at 3.30 p.m. and I showered, put on a suit, and left again 15 minutes later. Sue and I took a taxi through the Shanghai rush hour to a press conference with the British Council at the newly opened Rockbund Art Museum. By the time we sat down I was feeling pretty odd through lack of sleep, and the barrage of cameras and microphones didn't really settle my nerves. One of the council gave a rundown of the kind of cultural events we could expect to see at the UK Pavilion at the World Expo (the reason we were there).

My speech was short and to the point. I could tell you that this was because we like our music to speak for itself, but in fact it was because I was having trouble stringing a sentence together. We had a very small glass of wine afterwards, and then went to a local brewery where Sue pushed the culinary boundaries and had a Caesar salad, and I had pigeon (very nice, despite the fact that it was looking at me). I finally crawled into bed at midnight, a mere 24 hours after last being in bed.

Today we had a free day to get used to the time change, so despite it feeling early, I forced myself out of bed and took a cab to the Nanjing Road. Everybody seemed very friendly and, with a lot of tourists around, concerned for my personal safety. 'Watch bag!' was the refrain on every street corner. I clutched my bag tighter, the warning against pickpockets ringing in my ears, and

was a little disappointed when, five minutes later, the next concerned, civic-minded individual said, 'Watch, bag, DVD, T-shirt,
good quality.'

I wandered down the road to the Bund – a fantastic place
to walk, with a backdrop of the TV tower and some truly spectacular high-tech buildings. I was leaning on the railings when
someone tapped me on the shoulder. A man held out his camera,
pointed at me and the buildings and his friend, and smiled: the
universal sign for 'can you take a picture of me and my friend
against a backdrop of this iconic view, please?' I went to take the
camera, whereupon he pulled it away saying, 'No, no, no!' After
more miming I realized that he wanted a picture of me with his
friend. Still a bit groggy with jet lag, I agreed. He stood next to me
on the river bank, I watched my bag just in case, and we smiled.

Maybe he was at the press conference.

Thomas le Tank Engine and the lost ticket

A group of five of us, plus Mark Bamping (our tour manager
on this occasion), departed from St Pancras very early the other
morning. We were travelling to Luxembourg to perform a recital
for one of our major sponsors. As we have to fly so often, we took
the opportunity to travel by train; despite the fact that it took
longer, it seemed a much more civilized way to travel. However,
when my alarm went off at 5 a.m. after the concert in the Barbican
the night before, my thoughts were very uncivilized indeed.

There is a peculiar herd mentality that you develop when
you travel regularly with a group of a hundred people. It's like
being on a posh school trip (rather than a trip with a posh
school, which is something entirely different). It does, however,
gradually take away your independence and initiative: why
read the signs, when you can follow the luggage tag in front?

Last summer, when I got a little lost on the roads in France on holiday, I found myself looking around for assistance from Sue Mallet. On so many levels, this is most unhealthy.

So here were the six of us on the Eurostar to Brussels, which was quieter than normal until some card-playing teenagers arrived at Ebbsfleet; compared with the rest of the absent LSO, though, they were pretty tame. Once we had found the correct ticket office, we spent a pleasant hour drinking coffee on a wind-swept platform which obliged us with horizontal rain.

If you ever travel to Luxembourg from London, take my advice: go to Paris and then take the TGV. Don't go to Brussels and then take Thomas le Tank Engine. It took over three hours, which was significantly longer than the previous part of the journey, and stopped at at least three hundred stations. We had stopped five times before the names of the stations stopped saying Brussels.

Mark had given us some background information about the trip, including the warning that we should keep tickets from both parts of our journey for the entire day. It's this little nugget that the unseasoned traveller may dismiss as overly cautious. Turns out, it wasn't.

'*Bonjour. Votre billet, s'il vous plait.*'

We all fished around and presented our Eurostar tickets, and tickets for the Brussels-to-Luxembourg leg. Even Alastair Blayden's cello had its own ticket. Viola player Robert Turner, however, seemed to have mislaid his Eurostar ticket. It did seem a bit odd that, as well as tickets for the train we were on, they needed to see tickets for the train we had recently been on; it's not as if it's easy to stow away on the Eurostar, what with customs and all.

Robert did the universal mime for 'I'm looking for my ticket' while the guard waited impatiently. This consists of looking bemused at your own misfortune whilst patting every pocket, followed by a shrug of the shoulders. In reality, patting your pockets is an ineffectual way of finding a thin piece of paper. The guard told us he would come back in a few minutes, after Robert had found it. After a few more minutes of searching through music and newspapers, the ticket still hadn't appeared, but Mark produced a spare photocopy, which the guard accepted. After all the excitement, we fell asleep.

After another couple of hours we had passed into Luxembourg, where the customs officers walked through the train followed by two different guards. One of them looked like the Fat Controller, but was much less friendly. '*Billets!*' he demanded. We all groaned and found our tickets, which he checked thoroughly. As I looked out of the window I could see in the reflection the sight of Robert patting all his pockets and shrugging his shoulders. We all laughed, as he was obviously trying to lighten the mood. We knew he couldn't have lost the ticket, as he had had it checked and then fallen asleep, and we hadn't moved since. How can you lose a ticket when you haven't done anything?

He had lost the replacement ticket. We appealed to the better nature of the Fat Controller, but sadly he appeared not to have one. He took Robert's passport, as it was worth more on the black market than his viola. The atmosphere was becoming tense, and we all started patting our pockets as if we were doing some kind of ancient English folk dance. We pointed out that, even if the ticket had gone, we had already had it checked on this very train by a different guard. That seemed to help, so they went and found him. He remembered that Robert had mislaid it before and recounted the story that he had gone away and come back and that we had found the ticket and he had indeed checked it. This should have helped, as we now had proof from a guard that we had had the ticket for the train which we were no longer on.

But the Fat Controller was not happy. As he was from Luxembourg and the friendly guard was from Brussels, I think rivalry came into play. He suggested that Robert would have to go back to Brussels, or buy a new ticket. We all went into a pocket-patting frenzy, and Robert emptied his bag entirely in a desperate bid to keep the ensemble together. Mark had no more tickets except for the cello one, and they were unwilling to accept that; the passport was now in the Fat Controller's pocket; all seemed lost, when all of a sudden the old ticket appeared in ... Robert's wallet. We all cheered in a strange Continental way, a bit like those old Piat D'or adverts. The guard looked disappointed (as did Mark, which was a little strange). We got off the train and laughed about it as we sped in a taxi to the recital.

'I really thought we were going to have no viola for tonight at one point!' exclaimed Tom.

Mark piped up at the back, 'Oh, it would have been fine, actually. I play the viola, so I could have done it!'

There was silence in the cab.

Was this part of his plan all along? Had he resorted to underhand tactics just so that he could play the viola with the LSO? I bet he had *loads* of spare tickets in his bag.

3 Travel Arrangements
1912

O nce Warren Fales was involved with the LSO's US tour, plans moved quickly. He instructed his solicitors, Shipley & Co., to write to the board of the LSO confirming a guarantee of £900 for the trip. It would be held until 'satisfactory evidence' was shown 'that the orchestra and Herr Arthur Nikisch had departed for America'. A month later, another letter arrived in which Shipley & Co. intimated that they were in possession of a further £1,000 in connection with the American tour, which they were prepared to pay at the appropriate time.

The orchestra's confidence in its own abilities is clear to see in the discussions that went on. Although money was tight, the LSO was still negotiating hard to get the conditions they wanted, demanding a porter to move their baggage in addition to the one they were bringing, and $1,000 a day for the services of the orchestra. Pew agreed to the fee, and promptly made sure that he got his money's worth by arranging for the orchestra to give two concerts on at least half of the days. In the space of five days in the middle of the tour the LSO found themselves doing ten concerts, each in a different city.

The combination of the LSO, Pew, and Fales was a magnet for headlines; the pre-publicity hyped up the general public and irritated the press, particularly in Boston. But one idea nearly ended the venture before it began. In 1912, there was only one way to get to America, and so Thomas Busby found himself trying to negotiate a favourable deal with ocean-liner companies for the orchestra's passage. His idea involved the agreement of reduced ticket prices in return for the orchestra playing a few concerts on board ship.

The patronage of the King had given the whole enterprise a veneer of glamour and importance and, in what should have been a magnificent publicity coup, the ever-vigilant managing director had noticed that the proposed dates for the tour coincided with the maiden voyage of the much-heralded White Star liner, *Titanic*. The two biggest and most opulent liners of the day, *Titanic* and *Olympic*, were being built at the Harland and Wolff shipyard in Belfast. Although the latter was launched in June 1911, her bigger sister ship *Titanic* wasn't due to leave on her maiden voyage until March 20th 1912, a perfect fit for the LSO tour. As everything slotted into place, Busby was delighted with his plans: securing the finest conductor in the world, being the first European orchestra to travel to the USA, winning the King's patronage, and then, as the final flourish, arriving with maximum exposure and fanfare and as much free publicity as he could wish for into New York Harbor on the most famous ship ever to be built, *Titanic*.

Six months before the orchestra was due to leave, disaster struck. The *Olympic* was sailing in the safe waters of the Solent when she collided with HMS *Hawke*, a navy destroyer on exercise. Insurance pictures of the incident show a huge hole ripped in the side of the *Olympic*, and the damage to the warship was such that a new bow had to be made. There had already been problems with the size of the White Star liner when it had first docked in New York. She was much bigger than the other ships, and fairly cumbersome to manoeuvre, which had caused damage to other boats when docking. This incident, however, put her out of action and, as *Titanic* hadn't yet been fitted out, the White Star Line was desperate to get *Olympic* back into service as quickly as possible. Because of its size, accommodating passengers from the abandoned voyages to America was problematic, and consequently the workforce fitting out *Titanic* was ordered to repair the damage to *Olympic* as quickly as possible. All work on *Titanic* stopped for around three weeks, and several important parts – including the propellor shaft from *Titanic* – were used to replace damaged ones on *Olympic*.

Because of the delay in finishing off *Titanic*, in October 1911 the White Star Line Company was forced to revise the date of

Members of the LSO aboard the liner *Baltic*.

the maiden voyage to 10th April, exactly three weeks later than planned. This was a disaster for Busby and the LSO, as this new departure date was well into the first leg of their tour. Busby was forced to make alternative arrangements, and in December 1911 confirmed that the orchestra would now have to leave slightly earlier due to being forced to travel on a slower vessel, the White Star ship RMS *Baltic*.

Unlike the directors of the company, none of the players was aware of the original travel plans, but Busby cannot have been pleased that a brilliant piece of his jigsaw puzzle was lost. After delivering the LSO safely to New York on April 6th, the *Baltic* made its way back to Liverpool, arriving ten days later. Halfway back, on April 14th, 1912, it sent this message:

> Greek steamer *Athenia* reports passing icebergs and large quantities of field ice today in latitude 41°51'N, longitude 49°52'W. Wish you and *Titanic* all success. Commander.

4 A Long Way From Home
2012

A birthday, Mozart, and the importance of the LSO noticeboard

When you go away a lot, as we do in the LSO, it can get a little lonely at times. This may seem odd given that we travel in a large group, but there you have it. In a huge place such as New York, for instance, you can spend a free day on your own without bumping into anyone from the orchestra. On some days, this is most welcome, but making arrangements to meet up at a particular time takes on great importance, especially when people forget their mobiles. To aid the communication process, every hotel we stay at has a noticeboard in the foyer with notes from the management about where to go, maps, flight times, time changes, and usually some graffiti from a late-night excursion. It's nothing glamorous, just one of those flip charts that people in proper jobs use to show fiscal figures and product quota predictions (whatever they are).

We've now had some time to get over the jet lag. A lot of people have used some (or all) of this time to go shopping. This has clearly been noted by the management, as when I came down this morning there was a red notice on the board. Red means important in the world of management, perhaps a hangover from schoolteachers' marking schemes. The notice is a reminder that the luggage allowance for our flight to Chicago is only 23 kilos – a hint, maybe, that you might like not to buy that extra present or litre of expensive shampoo, or your excess baggage allowance will be huge.

Tonight we had the first concert of our New York City series. It's a concert we did in London, the Mozart Piano Concerto No. 27 and the *Requiem*. Mozart neglected to write for flutes in the *Requiem*; I'm sure he meant to, but had other things on his mind at the time. He never got round to telling Süssmayr to bung a couple of flutes in on top of the basset horns, especially during the bits about angels, either. I was, however, in the concerto – and what a concerto it is. It's a challenging way to start a concert, going straight into a concerto, but the Avery Fisher Hall makes it very easy to hear the piano from where I sit. I could also see the soloist's hands, which really helps.

A great performance was finished off when Sir Colin came back on stage and was presented with the biggest birthday cake I've ever seen. We all played 'Happy Birthday', of course, and the wonderful London Symphony Chorus sang too. It sounded terrible. It always does; it's traditional. I have seen Sir Colin presented with three cakes this year, and that's not counting the one he probably had at home in private. He has had at least three birthdays in different countries. That's more than the Queen.

I listened to the rehearsal of the Mozart *Requiem*, one of my favourite pieces. The choir and orchestra together sounded awesome, particularly in the *Dies Irae*, where I was worried the roof was going to cave in. John Stenhouse and Chi-Yu Mo were playing basset horns (the embarrassing uncle of the clarinet world), which sounded ethereal, as did Dudley Bright's wonderful trombone solo. The singers sounded good in the rehearsal, but it really is the choir who steals the show in this piece for me. They sound fabulous, and I'm looking forward to sitting in front of them when we do the *Creation* later on this week.

Just as we were about to rehearse this evening I had a text message from an old friend, who asked if I was in NY with the LSO. Nick Finlow is a musical director in the West End; we shared a house at college, and he was my best man and I was his. He's working on a musical on Broadway this week and, by chance, staying in the same hotel as us. At least, he *was* staying in the same hotel, until he saw his room and promptly decided

Chi-Yu Mo and John Stenhouse warm up their basset horns before playing Mozart's *Requiem* in New York.

to go somewhere nicer. As he was checking out in the foyer this afternoon he spotted the LSO noticeboard. The long and the short of it is that, thanks to the noticeboard being in the right place at the right time – and because Mozart neglected to write for flutes, which meant I finished early – I am having a drink with one of my best friends, in Manhattan. So, I won't be lonely after all.

New York, New York: it's a hell of a town.

Paris in springtime – or autumn

I can never remember whether Paris is the city *for* lovers or the city *of* lovers – it's a subtle difference but nonetheless an important one. In one scenario, loved-up couples stroll through the grand boulevards hand in hand; in the other, singletons constantly fend off the unwanted advances of desperate Lotharios ... I guess it's the city *for* lovers, before you start complaining. It certainly was when I was here for the first time in 1995, on my honeymoon. We didn't have very much money, and my wife and I walked for hours, stopping at museums, galleries, and shops, all interspersed with cups of coffee at pavement cafés.

Sadly, today I am wandering the streets of this beautiful city on my own. It's a funny thing, being on tour. While I feel lucky to have free days in Tokyo, New York, and Paris, it's not the same without the person you really want to share it with. No offence to my colleagues in the band, but I don't want to stroll along the Left Bank arm in arm with them, or climb the Eiffel Tower and gasp at the romance of the view. Therein lies the truth behind the glamour: Paris is a great place but, like all big cities, it can be lonely. Still, I am enjoying having yet another coffee before the concert as I write. The café is right outside the Salle Pleyel, where we have a residency, and it is called, believe it or not, the Do-Re-Mi.

Last night we played the quickest version of Prokofiev's Classical Symphony yet. When Valery came back on stage for the second time, he looked over at the woodwind section and a huge grin appeared on his face – I think he enjoys seeing how far he can push us. After the stage move we performed the Second Piano Concerto with Vladimir Feltsman – what a showman! He came on dressed all in black with very short white hair, looking not dissimilar to a pint of Guinness, and played like a man possessed. The piece is quite heavily orchestrated, and the soloist really has to fight to get through the texture. There are three or four long cadenzas, one of which Feltsman played with such passion that as his left hand thundered down towards the bottom of his instrument, he raised his right hand in a fist and shook it menacingly at the audience. Thank goodness nobody had any noisy sweet wrappers; I would have feared for their safety. He was so involved with the performance, it was a pleasure to watch as well as listen to.

At the end of the piece, there is a sudden quickening of tempo, and the piece finishes with a very fast repeated figure rushing up to a final *forte* chord. Feltsman played this final chord with such force that he literally leapt out of his seat with his arms outstretched in one movement. He continued across the piano to shake hands with Valery, almost as if it was written in the score – fantastic. The audience loved it, and called him back on repeatedly until he gave them an encore. I have no idea what it was, as my knowledge of piano pieces stopped after grade 4. I can say, though, that it must have been at least grade 7.

After the show, most people went for something to eat around the hotel. It had been a long day, and it was too late to start running around Paris. As we come here quite a lot, players often end up going to the same bars and restaurants; I could probably recite the menu for the Terminus Nord brasserie off by heart. But tonight, several people on my table at one of the low rent/high price cafés opposite the Gare du Nord ended up eating egg and chips.

I guess I'm not the only one who misses home.

It's a day off at last

We have now reached the halfway point of our tour. It feels a little calmer now that we're staying in Tokyo for a few days: it gives the orchestra a chance to stretch its legs, unpack its suitcases and, most importantly, not spend every waking hour in each other's pockets. Today is the first day off we have had on tour. In fact, I can't remember the last day off we had, as the band was playing in the Barbican the day before we left.

Back home at Château Davies in sunny Surrey, it is the birthday of my two boys. We had the party before I left for Japan, and late last night we all marvelled at the brilliant invention that is Skype. I chatted to them for two hours, and we could see each other on the webcam too. We all agreed that it was fabulous and almost the same as being there. But it wasn't. I would give up a lifetime of days off in Tokyo to be at home today.

Still, there was no point in sitting around being miserable, and it was beautiful outside, so I caught the tube to Ginza earlier and started wandering around to see what I could find.

The main road is a bit like Regent Street in London, except every spare bit of space is used. What looks like a department store is often about six shops piled on top of one another, selling anything from musical instruments to women's underwear. I went into a CD store, which also sells musical instruments, to have a look for anything different from the stuff we have back home. When you walk into a shop anywhere in Japan the staff all bow and say, or more often shout, a greeting which translates roughly as 'You are here!' This happens in all shops and restaurants, from the smallest corner shop to the largest department store. On this occasion, I was spotted as I walked in and the staff all shouted at me in unison like a chorus from a Greek tragedy. It made me jump, but their ensemble was excellent: you could tell it was a music shop.

I went up to the third floor (more shouting), and found the CDs. There were posters for our concerts, and seemingly hundreds of posters of Lang Lang, and quite a lot for Sarah Brightman. I was looking for some old Jean-Pierre Rampal recordings which he made for the Japanese market years ago. Rampal, if you don't know, was one of the great flautists from last century, and he loved Japan and food. His biography is a fascinating read as it does briefly mention the flute and music, but goes into minute detail about the food he ate on his travels. In fact, Sharon Williams, our piccolo player, owns a guide to sushi in Tokyo with a foreword written by the great man himself.

I found the instrumental recital section and started to look, but there was a problem. If you go into your local CD retailer in the West, all the CDs are facing outward so that you can see the picture on the front. In Japan they file them on the shelves like books in a library, with the spines facing outward. All of the writing is in Japanese, of course, and so unless you speak the language, it's a bit like a lucky dip. I didn't even know where the flute section was. I picked some out at random and came up with 'Orchestral Organ Fanfares', Japanese folksongs for the clavichord, and a guitar CD of an unfamiliar German composer. I never did find any flute CDs, and it was getting embarrassing, so I left. More shouting.

Out in the bright sunshine once again, I headed for the Tokyo beer hall, a place I had passed many times but never been into. It was built in 1934 (which makes it a very old building in

Tokyo), and the inside is covered in mosaics of Japanese interpretations of German scenes. The ceilings are huge, vaulted wooden structures which do bear a resemblance to German beer halls. The menu is a strange mix of Asian and Bavarian cuisine (wurst and wasabi with miso soup on the side, for instance) and about twenty types of locally produced beer. Most of the Japanese people in there seemed to be drinking a very dark stout, so I ordered one too. It was a bit like Guinness, but sweeter and very nice indeed, especially when my seafood noodles arrived. There was traditional German music playing: accordions and oompah bands, but with Japanese vocals. As my German isn't much better than my Japanese, I still had no idea what they were singing about. All in all, it was a bit like a surreal dream. I left to some more shouts, uncoordinated this time, and stepped from the darkness of the beer hall into the bright sunshine.

I went to the Tokyo toyshop, which at the moment is full of kitsch Christmas stuff, and bought a few bits and pieces for the kids. I ended the day wandering round Akihabara, which is known as the electronic district. In the daytime it doesn't look too impressive, but at night it is a sea of neon, making Piccadilly Circus look like a 10-watt eco-friendly bulb. The funny thing is that most of the signs are adverts, but apart from the obvious electric company signs, the rest are in Japanese and consequently are rather beautiful. They can't sell me something if I don't know what it is. Probably. I spent a couple of hours just walking and watching, until my feet started to hurt and I went back to the hotel.

By the time I got back from dinner, it was time to phone home again and see how the birthday boys were. Of course, by this time it was afternoon in Surrey, and they had eaten cake and generally been spoiled. My in-laws were round, my parents had been round, and my brother was arriving later. They all said how fantastic it was to be able to see me on the computer screen, and how it was almost like being there. But it wasn't.

A day off in an exciting, faraway city; lavish receptions; the best concerts of my life. But today, what I really want is some birthday cake.

The roaring silence

The speed at which we travel around the world nowadays belies the distances covered. It doesn't take that long to get from London to New York, and consequently it doesn't feel that far away. I imagine that spending ten days on a boat in 1912 must have given the players plenty of time to think about just how far away from home they were. Although it is now quicker to get here, and the city has changed a great deal since Turner and Nisbet visited, it is still the same distance from London.

According to his diary, it was almost two weeks into the tour before Turner received his first letter from home. When I first started touring I used to send postcards home, but I can't remember the last time I did; similarly, I remember only a decade ago, every night when we were in Japan, a long queue would snake around the hotel foyer as people waited in line to use the public telephone for their precious three minutes before the card ran out. In 2012, we don't have to wait for weeks for a letter; we don't even have to queue for the phone any more. In fact, I don't even have to leave my hotel room since Skype appeared.

When I'm in New York, I always seem to call home around teatime in the Davies household because of the time difference, and this time was no different. Because I had a new shiny laptop, however, I decided to show off to my kids and call them from a coffee shop with wifi that I was passing, mainly so that I could have the Empire State Building behind me in the image they would see at home. But things never quite work out as you want them to.

Picture this: my daughter is waiting for her tea and playing with the BBC children's website, making 'cyber bread', which I am told she has just put in the oven. My daughter guards her time on the computer fiercely, as she has to share it with her two bigger brothers. As she is sitting happily playing, Skype pops up and my face appears on her screen, automatically closing down her bread-making program. I can at this point see her on my laptop screen.

'Hello darling, it's Daddy, how are you? Are you being a good girl? I've missed you.'

She screams and starts having a tantrum (she's five), but manages to say, 'Daddy! I've waited ages to play on this and now your head's stopped my bread and it's not fair.'

She then runs off in a huff.

I guess it's a good thing that she isn't missing me as much as I am missing her. Thankfully, she did regain her composure, and we had a chat later on which made me walk around New York City with a spring in my step, not feeling so alone any more.

I felt alone again today, although in a room full of about two thousand people. It was on stage, in concert at the Lincoln Center. Tonight we played *Das Lied von der Erde*. Typically, Mahler orchestrates the huge forces so that at times the singers are pitted against the full force of the LSO, and at other times he thins the texture so that one solo line weaves around the soloists. I have one of those lines and, boy, does it feel lonely.

I have noticed the sensation before when playing *Prelude à L'Après-midi d'un faune*; the silence surrounding you is deafening. When we rehearsed *Das Lied*, it was the first time I had played it in my life. This is scary when conductor Bernard Haitink is standing in front of you – I mean, he knows how it's supposed to go, for goodness' sake. I had done my homework, and the solo cadenzas with the mezzo fitted. If you don't know the part I'm referring to, it's a couple of moments which involve just the cellos holding a low note very quietly indeed, and then the flute and mezzo weave a sinuous thread around each other until just the flute is left to descend gradually into nothingness. It can be a spectacular moment, but is absolutely terrifying to pull off in concert, when there are two thousand people watching and listening and the orchestra is still, hardly daring to breathe.

You don't notice in rehearsal, when people are moving around, coughing, writing things in their music; it takes a lot of effort actually to be quiet, and it never happens until the show. It was quiet this evening, with the polished hush of Avery Fisher Hall; as the four bars before my bit gradually became almost inaudible, the silence pressed in on my ears like sleep and I felt totally alone. It's an oppressive silence, during which everything around you seems to stop. A bit like when you wake up early in the morning – it's quiet, but just normal quiet. You can hear the leaves on the trees, the cars going past, and life humming away already without you. That is like the rehearsal. And then there are those mornings when you wake up early and there has been a heavy snowfall – a really deep quiet. The snow absorbs the sounds of the cars and leaves, and until you open the curtains, you can't be sure that someone hasn't removed the rest of the world from outside your window. That is what it feels like before I play the cadenzas – everything goes quiet, and my colleagues around me don't move or breathe in case they make a noise – there is a brief pause after the descending scale, and then we are off again to the end.

It's a wonderful, lonely moment. One of many for me in New York City.

5 The Men and Woman of the London Symphony Orchestra 1912

On Thursday 28th March 1912, the LSO assembled at Euston Station to catch the train to Liverpool. An article from the *Daily Sketch* shows a very crowded platform as all 96 men and one woman leave for the New World, surrounded by family and well-wishers. To modern eyes they look quite a sight, with everybody in suits, ties, overcoats, hats, and luxurious moustaches. All except the one female member of the orchestra, of course. Women? In the LSO?

In a remarkable 1970 book called *To Speak for Ourselves*, a collection of interviews with players from the orchestra, one of my predecessors, Peter Lloyd, was asked if he had any comment on the small matter that the LSO was the last orchestra in England not to include women. He said, 'Yes, I think that I would rather the LSO remained as it is. It is a more professional outfit as it is. Women can be a distraction.'

Back in 1904, however, a founder member of the orchestra was harpist Miriam Timothy. She had played in the Queen's Hall

Orchestra, and left to join the new LSO. Born in Peckham in 1879, she studied the harp in London, very quickly establishing herself as one of the most in-demand players in town. Miriam Timothy was well ahead of her time, and not content to be seen and not heard. She concentrated on her career until the age of 46, when she married and moved with her husband, Col. R. 'Bobby' Deane CBE, to his new job as commissioner of police in Mauritius. She never played in London again.

In a 1950 obituary* she is described as a 'very charming girl and a bright and outstanding star in the orchestra, also a personality which struck one as being fine and of a sweet and serious disposition, together with great fun and freshness – a perfect lady'. Miriam was a member of the orchestra until her marriage, and the obituary ends rather poignantly: 'She sold her harps just before she got married.' We also know that during her bars of rest, she used to do a considerable amount of knitting. These days, knitting needles are forbidden on aeroplanes, but I imagine that on that morning in 1912, Miriam Timothy had quite a number with which to occupy herself during a journey that would see the LSO covering over 12,000 miles.

The LSO, as is usually still the case, was travelling apart from its conductor, Arthur Nikisch, who would be arriving a day later on the RMS *Caronia*. The gossip columns in New York were already buzzing about his return to the States, calling him 'the $1,000-a-day conductor'. Board minutes reveal that the gossip was true: Nikisch had indeed accepted an offer of $1,000 a day, plus accommodation (albeit mostly on a train) and food. In today's money, over the course of the tour, this would equate to roughly $500,000. No wonder Pew was so glad to see Fales finance the tour: the 97 musicians of the LSO cost the same per

---

* Found at http://www.martinfamilyhistory.co.uk/DT2.htm

DAILY SKETCH, FRIDAY, MARCH 29, 1912.

LONDON SYMPHONY ORCHESTRA OFF TO AMERICA.

Great interest was taken by people in the Metropolis yesterday in the departure of the London Symphony Orchestra for a short tour in the United States. The tour opens in New York on the 8th of next month, and Boston, Philadelphia, Washington, Baltimore, and many other towns will be visited. The orchestra, which will be under the conductorship of Mr. Arthur Nikisch, numbers a hundred. The photograph shows the crowd on Euston Station yesterday just before the musicians' train left.

Some of the principals: Mr. E. Maney, conductor at Margate; Mr. E. F. James, chairman; Mr. P. Lewis, conductor at Rhyl; and Mr. T. R. Basby, secretary. — *Daily Sketch* Photographs.

The LSO's departure from London, as reported by the *Daily Sketch*.

day as their conductor. Nikisch did work hard for his money, however, and courted the American public by means of several articles in the *New York Times*.

'NIKISCH HAS ONE REGRET' was the headline on March 31st:

> Every human being makes one great mistake in his lifetime, and I realize more and more every day how stupid I was that I ever left America. I am looking forward with extreme pleasure to my visit. I have retained a splendid memory of my four years with the Boston Symphony Orchestra, and I enjoyed immensely the artistic interest of the American people, even in the smallest cities, in the best class of music.

And so the publicity machine continued to grind away, always mentioning Nikisch's association with the great orchestras of the world, and expanding on his regret at ever having left the States. The *New York Times* of March 3rd 1912 quoted him as saying:

> I am looking forward to it with the kenest [*sic*] joy and artistic anticipation. It is so pleasant for me to hear that my revisit to the United States is awaited with so much eagerness and sympathy. I am making the statement without exaggeration when I say that those four years I stayed in America as the conductor of the Boston Symphony Orchestra were, thanks to the kindness, appreciation, and enthusiasm of the American public, perhaps the very happiest time of my artistic career. I am delighted to go back at the head of one of the finest orchestras in the world.

This wonderfully crafted piece of PR ended with a question for the maestro. He was asked what changes he expected to find in the United States. He replied: 'I hope none at all, for the treatment I received there cannot be surpassed.'

Marvellous! However, the constant references to Boston and Berlin in the weeks preceding the tour would eventually turn against him – and the orchestra – as constant comparisons were made, and not very favourably to begin with.

As Nikisch was packing his trunk, the LSO was on the train to Liverpool. Owing to the huge number of people on the platform waving them off, and presumably the formidable amount of luggage, it was delayed; some things never change. Charles Turner describes that first day:

> Arrived safe at Liverpool, a little late. Saw mother but only had time to speak and was ushered on board anyhow. Mother saw us slowly steam away. I waved my hat a long time. We had dinner about 7.30 and everybody seemed to enjoy it. Got fixed up in cabin which is our home for the week. Schroeder, Merry (percussion section) and myself. The sea was like a lake and cannot feel any motion. Retired about 12 p.m. and had a bad night owing to my asthma troubling me.

After reaching Queenstown early on Friday morning, they set sail for America. For the next few days, the situation on board the smaller *Baltic* was less desirable. The sea became rough, and most of the orchestra were unwell.

> 29 March: We have dinner at 6 p.m., the last meal, for a time, for a good many including myself. By 7 o'clock the sea is rough. The ship's chart says 'rough head sea'. I, of course, retire about 7.30 and shoot the cat [vomit] and get into bed. I find that if you be perfectly still the motion of the boat does not worry you – with my asthma I cannot lie still so am in a nasty fix and pass a rotten night.

As Turner says, many of the players didn't adjust well to the boat. Henry Nisbet is a little more to the point: 'When we had got away about 40 miles, the ocean became a bit rough and several of our boys gave up the Ghost, I mean "shot the cat".'

For the next few days the passengers tried to contain their meals, and cats continued to be shot, although on the Tuesday a live stowaway cat was finally caught after making a nuisance of itself in the cabins and was executed through a porthole over a thousand miles from land. The ship was packed to capacity, as the White Star Line had been forced to accommodate passengers on alternative routes because of the *Titanic* delay, and conditions were not ideal. The LSO took up the main portion of the second-class cabin but, according to Nisbet, in the lower-class area things were far from comfortable: 'There are 1500 steerage passengers of almost every nationality, and [they] are packed up like sardines on their small deck, it is very pathetic to see them so mixed up, some quite nicely dressed people, and others fearfully ragged.'

Unlike the cruise ships of today, the *Baltic* provided only basic entertainment. There were musical evenings, readings, and sports days. On April Fool's Day, of all days, sports were organized on deck. Whether because they were violent, the sea was rough, or the players were very competitive, the orchestra suffered several injuries. Nisbet sprained his leg after three races and retired from competition; E. Maney, one of the first violinists, overexerted himself and was put to bed by the doctor with a strain on the heart; and the worst of all was Joe Field, one of the cellists. He slipped on the deck, broke his kneecap, and was confined to a hospital in New York for the duration of the trip. The LSO was one man down before they even arrived.

6 Planes, Trains, and Automobiles (and Bicycles, and Running)
2012

Bernard, Bruckner, and bikes

As we approach the end of what feels like a long season of concerts, I cannot think of a more satisfying way to finish than with Bernard Haitink on the podium. All conductors have different styles, whether dancelike, quivering, rude, tormented genius, or extended baton (others are available). Bernard is one of a precious few who don't really seem to do anything much when they stand in front of an orchestra.

Let me clarify that straight away: less is more. I am positive that as Haitink has grown older, as with Sir Colin, economy of effort has influenced his conducting style; but with an orchestra like the LSO, alert to every twitch of an eyebrow, large expansive gestures are simply unnecessary. They are probably for the audience's benefit – this is theatre, after all. However, Bernard doesn't always say very much, either. He doesn't need to: it's all there in his movement, before he opens his mouth or indeed his score.

As it is nearly the end of term, the orchestra can be a noisy environment in which to work, and I'm not talking about the violas cowering in front of the trumpets. There is a level of acceptable chatter which is almost always vibrant discussion of musical points. I can speak only for the flute section, but assume that it is the same in the horns. There are many occasions during rehearsals when Lennie MacKenzie, the chairman, has to shush the orchestra so that we can listen to the pearls cast before us – but with Bernard, there is no need for this. At the start of the rehearsal, he stands in front of us looking around at who is on the stage, smiling at old friends, nodding at new ones. The orchestra smiles back and is silent. He speaks: 'So. Good morning. Bruckner 4, yes?'

He sweeps his gaze across the string section and a small flick of his baton coaxes the warmest sound I have ever heard from them. He smiles. He looks up to David Pyatt in the horn section, and with another flick that famous call is plucked from the air. Bernard encourages a little more sound with his left hand before the woodwind section echoes the opening motif. The acoustic in the Barbican is a little dry compared with Salle Pleyel in Paris, but the orchestra sounds rich, dark, and different from when any other conductor is playing with us. Gradually you can sense his left hand starting to move slightly more, not that you could tell from the audience, but we can sense it from the stage. The first of the monumental crescendos has begun: a slight bloom in the sound at first, but gradually the depth of sound becomes more powerful with each bar, inevitable and unstoppable. The final four bars before the first of many peaks in this piece approaches. Bernard slowly raises his left hand and lightly clenches his fist, which he shakes, and then as we reach the ff marking he subdivides his beat into four without changing tempo. A slight flick of his shoulders and his fist comes slowly down with the weight of granite. The stick slices the air. The sound that is unleashed is huge, not just loud, but massive and wide and warm. Bernard takes in the faces of the orchestra. Everyone who doesn't blow something is smiling and sitting back in their chairs. He hasn't said or done anything that you would notice from the auditorium, and yet he has said and done everything. The sound of the LSO has changed in three minutes, and not a word has been said. This is a master at work.

After two concerts in the Barbican we found ourselves on the Eurostar early on Saturday morning. There seemed to be a vast number of instruments around. It turned out we were sharing the train with the Orchestra of the Age of Enlightenment, and a string quartet. Despite the recipe for a noisy journey, most people were tired, and slept or read the engorged Saturday papers before we arrived during a torrential downpour in Paris. It was one of those 'this isn't going to stop' storms, so we all (LSO and OAE) ran across to the same hotel by the station. As two orchestras tried to find room keys at the same time, we looked out of the door to see that the storm that wasn't going to stop had stopped, and the sun was shining.

Although we shared train and hotel, we had the hall to ourselves. Just as well, as the forces needed for the Bruckner are vast and cover most of the stage. Things were a little more intimate for the Mozart Piano Concerto, which we were playing with the wonderful Maria João Pires; in fact, the way she turned and reacted to the woodwind section in the conversational passages made me feel as if I were playing in a string quartet rather than an orchestra. (A string quartet with a flute, anyway. And a piano.) She was a joy to play with, and a perfect appetizer for the heavy Bruckner. We finished the balance rehearsal with Mozart as the stage was being set for the concert. Bernard turned to the soloist, 'So, we start and you play what you want, yes?'

'Yes, whatever you want, Maestro.'

We started the orchestral *tutti*, and the piano joined about four minutes into the piece. Bernard turned again and Maria João smiled back. They both shrugged their shoulders and stopped. 'OK?'

'Yes!'

'Anything else you would like to do?'

'I don't know. Maybe second movement?'

Bernard turned to the second movement. 'So which bit would you like to do?'

'Well, I don't mind, you say.'

Bernard paused and looked thoughtful. 'You know, I always hated these rehearsals right before a concert. It's the wrong temperature.'

He turned to the soloist once again, 'And you know you play very well. I have no criticisms!' She smiled, and the rehearsal ended. The concert an hour later was wonderful.

On our return to London we had a brief rehearsal before the final concert. Afterwards I was walking to the lift carrying my Brompton in its folded-up state. I met Bernard waiting for the lift, and he instantly spotted my hand luggage.

'Ah, a Brompton; very impressive, Gareth. Do you cycle all the way here on that?!' (I live 30 miles away.)

'No, it's only got two gears! Maybe if I had three?'

He laughed. 'You know, I have recently bought a new bicycle.' As he is Dutch, I suppose I shouldn't have been surprised, but it wasn't the conversation I was expecting to be having in a lift with Bernard Haitink. 'Yes, it's one of those bikes that has an electric motor on it! I still have to pedal, but it helps me get up the hills these days.'

'I expect you'll go flying past me, then, Bernard.'

'Oh I don't think so, Gareth! See you tomorrow.'

Bernard Haitink. Legend. Maestro. Cyclist.

What I think about when I think about playing

Autumn arrives late in Tokyo. The trees are still covered in red leaves which, in the early-morning sun, form a ring of fire around the Imperial Palace. The branches inside the closed-off section of the grounds are guarded by soldiers standing on gravel paths which alert them to the footfalls of intruders. The leaves fall unnoticed around them as they watch me run past. The previous evening we had driven to the concert on the other side of Tokyo and I had noticed that the pavements were crowded with runners of all ages in Day-Glo fabrics. It looked like there was a race on, but after a search on the Tokyo runners' forum, I discovered that it was just a popular time of day to run there.

Tokyo convention dictates that you should run anticlockwise around the Palace. Despite the lack of other runners at this early hour, I decide to be conventional and spend the next hour craning my neck to the left to look into the Royal enclave. There may not be many other people doing what I'm doing, but despite it being around 7 a.m., the pavements on the 2km run to get to the Palace are crammed with workers going into the government buildings near by. Unlike London, everybody stops at red lights and waits for the green man; the collective peer pressure is enormous, and I take a while to warm up, but once I reach the central area the views are spectacular. On one side of the Palace is a huge wall with lawns stretching out to the road dotted with precisely clipped trees. As I clock up the kilometres I reach the far side and find a huge moat, breathtaking in its depth. There is a light mist coming off the water and the surface is rendered silver by the sun.

I am still not sleeping well, despite having been here over a week. Running is the best cure, and I make my way back up to the hotel, dodging city workers as best I can. I was hoping to bump into Haruki Murakami, the author, as if you have read his wonderful book *What I Talk About When I Talk About Running*, you'll know he vividly describes running around the area and the people he sees every day. I realized pretty quickly that I had no idea what he looks like though, so I smiled at everybody just in case.

So what do I think about when I think about running? I don't think about running, otherwise I wouldn't do it; it hurts. I think about music, or more specifically the music I am working on at the moment. I do have an iPod, but I don't tend to run with it on unless I'm trying to learn some new music. When we did a Prokofiev tour last year, I ran to all the symphonies for a while to reacquaint myself with them. (If you are interested, I found No. 6 was just the right tempo a lot of the time and No. 1 was useful for getting up the hill on my way home.) Most of the time, though, my head is filled with noise, and I really don't need any more; I enjoy running away.

Today I have Mahler's 9th symphony on my mind, as when I get back from the Palace we have a rehearsal with Valery for the final concert of the tour. I think it is probably the hardest of his symphonies to bring off. Every time we play it, people are divided. Everyone seems to have a perfect version in mind, nobody ever fulfils all of the criteria, and so people are dissatisfied. If you search on Google for a preferred recording of the symphony you will find no consensus whatsoever: one version will have otherworldly qualities, one will be febrile, one chaotic but human, another perfect but clinical. I find this liberating. There is no strict method to adhere to. With Valery, there is no telling who it will please, but it certainly won't be clinical or dull. The symphony is a rollercoaster of a ride, taking the listener and performer from the modernist leanings of the first movement and the highs of the second to the bittersweet finale in which Mahler makes your world collapse around you, only to offer a shaft of light at the conclusion. I really don't know whether I enjoy playing it or not, but I always need a stiff drink afterwards.

Yesterday, after the rehearsal, we had a couple of hours to go and eat something. A few of us went next door to the Tokyo Dome complex, where there is a shopping centre with a rollercoaster on the roof. Japan is complex place, and never exactly what you expect. A rollercoaster in a shopping centre? Waiting for the green man? Whatever next? However, on a Sunday afternoon in Tokyo I can think of nothing better than to go out with a group of dear friends who know no fear, and go on one of the most thrilling white-knuckle rides known to man.

We are lucky to have Valery.

Taking coals to Newcastle

Autumn is encroaching quickly now. At 8 a.m., running along the Rhine for twenty minutes turns my hands to blocks of ice; I cast envious glances at the local runners, with their hats and gloves, smiling sympathetically as I suffer. Mad dogs and Englishmen.

When I set out this morning, it was impossible to see across the river to the other bank because of the thick fog. The sun was reduced to a dull circle in the distance and my breath vapour seemed to add to the heavy mixture. The bleep from my GPS watch every kilometre sounded muffled and apologetic. Down at the edge of the water there was a crescendo of noise as the waves suddenly increased in intensity and then silently, out of the mist, a ship appeared, momentarily pushing the water and fog apart. It reminded me of watching the trains coming out of the tunnel near my home station: the commuters coiled on the platform, pulses raised, counting the number of carriages as they come out of the darkness. Will it be twelve and the chance of a seat, or only eight and standing room if you're lucky? The ship

Valery Gergiev conducts the LSO in Japan.

kept on emerging from the darkness until, at last, the cabin cut through, and I could see just how vast it was. I say ship, but it was more like a huge barge, loaded from end to end with what looked like coal. By the time I reached the last part of my run, the sun had won and the thick fog was reduced to small wispy clouds tossed along the surface of the water. The temperature rose. It was time to go to work.

We were playing Beethoven in Bonn: taking coals to Newcastle, as the saying goes. As Beethoven was born and lived in Bonn, much like Mozart in Vienna/Salzburg, or Mahler or Strauss in Vienna, there are little bits of Ludwig all over town. You can visit the Beethoven Haus where he was born in 1770; you can see his last grand piano, his instruments for string quartets, and even his ear trumpets. Almost every shop you pass has an identical statue of Beethoven in his familiar, grumpy-faced pose. They are made from fibreglass and decorated in keeping with the shop they stand in front of. The one outside the jeweller's in the square has been painted to look like marble with a velvet hat on top, while the one at the ice-cream shop bears the colours of every single flavour they sell. Razumovsky Ripple, anyone?

We were here to play three concerts at a Beethoven festival: one with Sir Colin – *Missa Solemnis* – and the other two with Sir John Eliot Gardiner, playing symphonies 4 and 5, and the next night 1 and 9. It is always special playing Mahler in Vienna, or Debussy in Paris, and it is the same playing Beethoven in Bonn: excitement tinged with a little apprehension. His symphonies are cornerstones of Western music, works that evoke strong feelings. A lady who spoke to me before the show said, 'I have heard No. 5 so many times, as you can imagine! I am looking forward to seeing what you do with it.'

Fortunately for us, John Eliot is one of the most opinionated and knowledgeable people on Beethoven. We have been working with him in this repertoire for about four years now, and the style he requires for this music is now part of the orchestra's DNA. I'm always astonished at how flexible the orchestra can be, playing Beethoven with Colin or Bernard in one way, and then as soon as John Eliot is on the box, a switch is flicked and a very different animal stalks the stage. The whip-crack speed at which he takes the opening of the famous Fifth, the tension he creates, and the attack he demands all take something that has become a clichéd calling card for 'classical music' and turn it back into the rallying, forward-looking electric shock that it surely was when first played. But it's not simply playing things fast: the phrasing is challenging and flexible. There are no moments during John Eliot's concerts when I am not on the edge of my seat as he shapes a phrase with his left hand, or punches out hemiolas I had never noticed before.

As I looked out into the audience, in the front row there was a young boy wearing a top hat and a cravat; he looked as if he had dressed up for the occasion as Beethoven himself. Before the music started he was all fidgets and sweets, with his parents trying to keep him still. As soon as the music began, sound leapt off the stage, and every time I looked at the boy he was open-mouthed, unblinking, just staring at leader Roman Simovic's hands. The boy's sweets remained untouched in his lap.

As we pounded towards the end of the Fifth Symphony, John Eliot jabbed at the sections of the orchestra where the theme he wanted to hear would appear. I could hear him singing under his breath the words he says are behind the final triumphant theme: *la Liberté*. Free indeed. This was not Sunday-morning Beethoven, burbling away quietly, making a nice relaxing noise but not enough to disturb the calm of the day; this was the Beethoven who dedicated the *Eroica* symphony to Napoleon and then later withdrew it as a protest. This was the Beethoven who shook up the musical establishment and changed the direction of music. This was the Beethoven whose portraits have defined the look for generations of suffering composers. This was the Beethoven who grabs you by the scruff of the neck and forces you to listen.

The audience leapt to their feet at the end of the symphony and cheered. I could feel the adrenaline pumping around my body, and a sense of relief. Everyone on stage was smiling; everyone in the audience was smiling. We might have taken coals to Newcastle, but John Eliot's coal fizzes, pops, and burns more brightly than most.

Programme for one of the concerts on board the *Baltic* on the way to New York.

7 The First Concerts
1912

One of the conditions of the passage to America that Busby had managed to negotiate was that the LSO was to give some concerts on board RMS *Baltic*. These ranged from full orchestral events (in first class, which must have been rather cramped) to evening recitals of solo instruments and piano. The first of these was on Tuesday April 2nd. Charles Turner describes getting ready:

> We got into evening dress – a great nuisance – and played from 8.45 till about 10 pm. Went and sat on deck but felt sleepy and retired only to be woken many times during the night by the fog horn of the steamer. There are also plenty of late comers to bed. One party at 3 am.

The orchestra was finally finding its sea legs – just as well, as the next day, conditions took a turn for the worse.

> The ship is pitching and rolling rather severe. The waves break occasionally on the ship like big guns booming in the distance. We give a concert in 2nd class saloon tonight. Hope to be well enough to play. Down to dinner as usual at 5 pm. The soup is

all over the plate. Have a light dinner and lie down to prepare for the concert. The noise in the ship is terrific. Every board in the ship cracks and the everlasting throb of the engines makes a pandemonia [*sic*]. There is also the crying children. Poor little things must be bad as well as the big ones.

As conditions became worse that evening, Turner decided not to risk the performance.

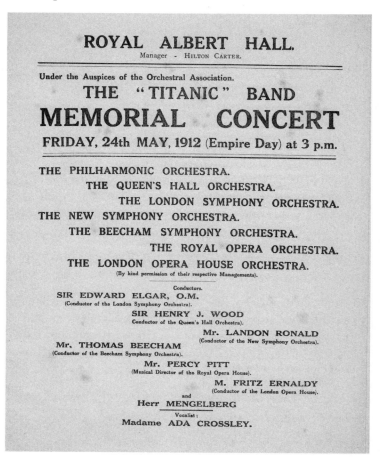

(Above and opposite) Posters for the *Titanic* Band Memorial Concert in London, in which the LSO took part after returning home.

I get ready for the concert at 7.45 but on getting in the corridor I think twice about it and give it up. I hand my sticks to Fred Merry (percussion) and go back to bunk. I don't want to take any chances. Not sick or anything but don't want to be. So be comfortable and listen to it in the distance. The boys finish and come along. I have a drop of brandy and undress. I turn in. Swap Schroeder my half bottle of whisky for his half bottle of brandy. Have a very good night only awake about twice and the rough sea still on.

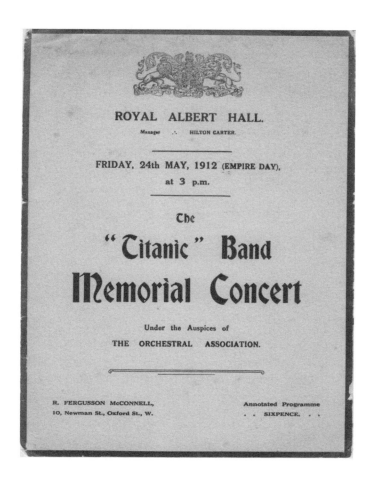

Fred Merry seemed to have a stronger constitution, and treated the second-class saloon to some timpani sight reading. The storm didn't abate during the concert, as Wynn Reeves, a first violinist, explained in his unpublished memoirs:

> After a day or two the orchestra settled down and decided to give a concert and in spite of a heavy sea was well attended. Arthur Payne, who conducted, supported himself with one arm round a pillar while the other held Miriam Timothy's harp. There were one or two awkward moments – the first oboe making a hurried exit in the middle of a solo ...

There was one more concert on board before the orchestra arrived in New York Harbor after ten days at sea. Perhaps somewhat prophetically, the concerts on board were for the Seamen's Charities in New York and Liverpool, and the South Holland and United States Life-Saving Institutions.

The LSO's next benefit concert would be on May 24th 1912 at the Royal Albert Hall, in aid of the *Titanic* Band Memorial Fund.

8 First Impressions
1912

N ew York City, the movie star, is so familiar now even to those who have never visited that it's difficult to imagine the impact on the LSO players of arriving there for the first time. As they stood on the deck of the *Baltic*, the Statue of Liberty must have been a welcome sight after ten days at sea. First impressions of the city were not entirely favourable: before they could get to their hotel, the entire orchestra with its baggage, instruments, and music had to be checked through customs. Turner notes:

> Awake about 3 or 4 am. Still dark. The engines are stopping and it disturbs me. We are getting into New York Harbour. Everybody up at 5 am shouting and larking. Breakfast 6 am – early rising this! We are a very long time landing and when we land lots of trouble with the baggage. They inspect it all. Everything must be opened. Go to Hotel Victoria, Broadway. Walk round in afternoon and dinner at 6 pm. Schroeder and myself have an amusing experience with some cabmen but we don't get quite taken in. The weather is as hot as it was in London last summer.

However, Henry Nisbet doesn't like it at all:

> Arrived at New York at 7.30 am, weather very hot, the first hot day this year, went to Victoria Hotel, nearly baked there through steam heating, walked along Broadway with Gomez in the morning; the town is quite rotten, streets much too narrow for the high buildings, roads & pavements in a disgraceful state of repair – trams ugly and overhead railway an awful disfiguration. Rehearsal at 7.30 pm.

Henry Daniel Nisbet, second flute player on the 1912 tour, in his Bandmaster uniform.

Charles Turner (timpani) and Fred Merry (percussion) on Brooklyn Bridge shortly after arriving in New York.

After a good night's sleep on solid ground (albeit with three other men sharing the room), Nisbet sees the city in a slightly more forgiving light:

> Went for a motor bus ride to ferryside with Gomez and Payne, through 5th Avenue the millionaires' residences were very fine indeed, but much too ostentatious. We nearly all have bad colds, I especially have a bad one; through the artificial heating one is subjected to chills so easily.

Turner seems to be enjoying himself a little more. He and the rest of the percussion section take a walk

> ... to Brooklyn Bridge, a gigantic affair over the mouth of the Hudson River. Nothing happens. Lunch at 1 pm. Then we go to the Zoological Gardens at Bronx Park. Ride all the way 35 or 40 minutes fast run on the subway for 5 cents. Commences to rain and eventually pours. We get home anyhow at 6 no worse. The Electric light advertising in New York at night is very novel and beautiful. Got a rotten cold in my head, but the asthma has gone altogether and I feel more free than I have for 12 months. I believe the voyage has cured me. Hope so.

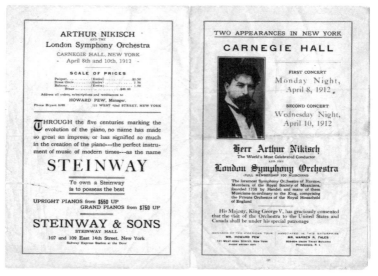

Flyer advertising LSO's appearances at Carnegie Hall with Arthur Nikisch.

The reaction from the players to their new surroundings was mixed, and the same could be said of critics' responses to the orchestra. After a blitz of publicity in the month before its arrival, expectations were running high for the band, which was being touted as the greatest orchestra in the world. The LSO arrived having not really played very much for two weeks, and after only two rehearsals in New York – one of which took place before Nikisch arrived – they took to the stage of Carnegie Hall for the first time on April 8th. Edgar Wilby, one of the second violins, said that the first sound of the orchestra in the hall came 'like an electric shock. It made one feel proud of oneself.'

The atmosphere at that first concert was tense and excited. Pew had set the scene for a night of legendary music-making, one that would linger in the minds and hearts of New Yorkers for a long time. The hyperbole had been noted by the *New York Times*:

After much heralding, the London Symphony Orchestra, with Arthur Nikisch at its head, appeared in New York last night in Carnegie Hall, giving the first concert of its American tour. The undertaking is a very large one, and it is not surprising that the enterprising managers should have exhausted the art of the press agent to advertise the enterprise they are conducting. Expectation was raised very high. The audience was very considerable in numbers, though it did not entirely fill the hall.

A good house, but, despite the manager's best efforts, not a sell-out. Nikisch was praised for his conducting and his profound musical interpretations, a welcome return for the great maestro. But what of the self-proclaimed 'best orchestra in the world'? It met with a mixed reception: the review praised the sound of the strings, although admitted that they had a brilliant sound rather than a mellow one. The wind players were quite good, the brass excellent:

The orchestra as a whole is exceedingly responsive to the conductor, but its ensemble, especially its attack, is not of the most finished. [The Brahms symphony] has not been heard more beautifully this season ... although there was one more technically finished. It was not only dramatically forceful, but musically convincing; at least for the moment.

Both our diarists seemed happy with the concert and the reception they received, although Turner grumbled: 'Not a very large audience. The concert goes very finely. I am unfortunate and break a good skin. This is a bit of bad luck for me. New drum head costs me $4.00.'

Critics were moderately impressed with the LSO. There was still talk of Nikisch's tenure with the Boston Symphony, and whether the two orchestras could be compared, but there would be another opportunity for New Yorkers to hear the orchestra in two days' time, at the second Carnegie Hall concert. Before that, on April 9th, the LSO boarded a train to Boston. Turner wrote: 'We have a 6 hour journey. They have a famous orchestra in Boston.

Hope we do well. I get my policy for insurance in case of accident.'

As it turned out, this insurance might well have come in handy after the mauling the orchestra received from Boston's critics. The people were to welcome Nikisch and his new band with open arms, but the press were waiting in the darkness of the stalls for their prey. They had sharpened their pencils and their tongues, and weren't afraid to use them.

9 America
2012

The one where we arrive in New York

What I dislike most about going on tour to America is queuing for a work visa at the American Embassy in London. It's not the hours of waiting: I often bump into old friends there who I haven't seen for years, and it's a good time to star-spot: last time I was behind Jamie Cullum (actually, I nearly trod on him, he's so tiny). Sharon Williams, our piccolo player, was next to none other than Sporty Spice in the queue; she said it was almost worth getting up for.

No, the worst part is the visa photos. They cost ten pounds, and you can use them only once because they are slightly bigger than those required by any other country. I have a new visa roughly every six months, which, apart from making a dent in my finances, forces me to watch myself ageing before my very eyes. My current passport is nearly full of visas. Remember when you were at school and you used to make flip books? I used to draw a little stick man in the bottom corner of an old exercise book, and on the next page draw the same man again, but slightly further along the page. When you'd finished the book, you could flip quickly through the pages and it looked as if the stick man was running along the book. If you flip through the pages of my passport quickly, you get a stop-frame animation of my gradual physical decline over the last few years. I'm thinking of fixing my old school photos onto the front of my passports when I retire and flipping through my entire life in about thirty seconds. Twenty-five to 65, just like that – which, I'm told by my parents, is pretty much how it feels anyway.

At the moment I am sitting on the bus from JFK Airport with the glistening lights of Manhattan dancing in the distance. It's 2.45 a.m. in London, and I'm a bit tired now, although it's only 9.45 p.m. here. One of my friends has informed me that the best way to beat jet lag is to stay up until midnight. We have a rehearsal tomorrow afternoon with pianist Imogen Cooper, for

The author on Brooklyn Bridge.

the Mozart Piano Concerto No. 27. It is a wonderful piece, with really great writing for the orchestra, and will sound wonderful in the crystal-clear acoustic of Avery Fisher Hall. We have to be out by five o'clock, as the New York Phil has a concert in the evening, so a group of us are taking advantage of the excellent exchange rate and having dinner at Gordon Ramsay's new restaurant. Even with the exchange rate, I fear I may have to resort to McDonald's by the end of the week. I'm off a for a quick nightcap and then bed. This city may never sleep – but I do.

Your name's on the list, but you ain't comin' in

Do you ever get the feeling that someone is watching you? I do. Obviously, on stage, I really am being watched; but I mean in everyday life.

American readers may not be aware that to get into that wonderful country we have to jump through hoops, queue in the rain for hours, queue some more and then give fingerprints, queue some more and then have a photo taken, queue, then smile and answer questions and fill in forms, and finally pay vast amounts of money in order to obtain a visa. Men aged 18–45 have a special supplementary form, with questions like 'Have you ever been involved in genocide?', 'Have you been involved in chemical training?', and 'Were you a member of the Nazi party in Germany?' (Chi, our principal E-flat clarinet player, is a Doctor of Chemistry, so he answers 'yes' to one of those, although genocide and fascism aren't really his style.)

We always go through this process in groups of ten or so, which is supposed to speed things up, but seems to have the opposite effect – at least, it does if Sharon is in the group. I don't want you to think she is disorganized – far from it – but every time she is in my group at the embassy, everything grinds to a halt. When we went a few weeks ago, it became clear why. The man behind the glass asked for some more information as her name was flagged up on their computers. It turns out that there are two other people called Sharon Williams, both of whom are on the FBI's 'Most Wanted' list. She assures me that she is neither of these people.

I have noticed a look of recognition on the faces of the audience when we play one of the encores on this trip. As soon as the opening bars of the March from *The Love for Three Oranges* starts, people look at one another and laugh. Now, I know the concept of being in love with even one orange is a bit weird, but it doesn't explain this reaction. Valery, having brought the orchestra and audience to their feet several times, rushes back on stage; in one sweeping movement he bows, turns to face the orchestra, whips his hands round like a discus thrower and launches the full fury of the trumpet section, followed by stratospherically high oboes. It sounds angular and odd, not the kind of music to bring a smile to one's face.

My sources tell me, however, that this passage used to be the theme tune of a radio programme about the FBI in peace and war. In the dark days of the Cold War, I suppose the irony of a Russian conducting a piece linked to the FBI would have sent a shiver down the spines of certain audience members, but we're all friends now – apart from Sharon, who is quite clearly being kept under surveillance by dark forces. The long history of hidden codes in music, from Mozart's three-chord Masonic calls to Shostakovich and his constant *DSCH* utterances, is being continued in our encore. I'm sure I saw a couple of guys in suits and sunglasses reach for their earpieces as soon as they heard our signal. I've suggested Sharon starts checking into hotels under a false name and sweeping her rooms for bugs.

When we were in Chicago two days ago, there was a notice

backstage listing suggestions for repertoire: pieces that musicians had proposed as ideas for the coming seasons. It made fascinating reading. Some of it was standard rep in Britain – Elgar, Vaughan Williams – but there were other pieces and composers I had never heard of. I thought I'd leave a suggestion of my own. I wrote, 'The theme from *Cagney & Lacey*.'

If you happen to see the Chicago Symphony Orchestra next time they play in London, listen out for their encore just in case they use my suggestion. I can sense the satellite dishes at GCHQ bristling with anticipation already.

The flute? Awesome!

'You haven't filled in the green form, sir,' said the man at Immigration.

Here we go again, I thought.

'Oh, I'm sorry, I see you have a work visa, so you don't have to fill in the green form, just the white and blue ones – it's just that most folks come here on holiday. I haven't seen many work visas.'

We had landed at Orlando Airport, a tourist rather than a business hub. The man was very friendly, but I was tired, and answering questions was not high on my to-do list.

'So you're here with the London Symphony? Cool!'

I knew what was coming next.

'And what instrument do you play?'

If had a dollar for every time I had been asked that at an airport, I would retire. It's not that I mind being asked; it's the response I get when I say that I play the flute. It's normally along the lines of 'That's for girls', or 'I used to play the recorder', or even 'Are you gay, then?' Sometimes I say that I play something manly, like the trumpet, but my bag gives me away.

'I play the flute,' I say with a big cheesy grin, and await the abuse.

'Awesome,' he says.

'I'm sorry?'

'Awesome! It's awesome that you play the flute, man. Have a great trip.'

I am stunned into silence, smile, and walk off with testosterone in my step feeling ... well ... awesome. Nobody has ever told me that the flute is awesome before. Ever.

The hills are alive with the sound of Prokofiev

The hills of San Francisco are short and sharp, but the views after a lung-busting climb are spectacular. I decided to explore the city on foot rather than catching one of the famous cable cars. I came out of the hotel and walked up Hyde Street, which undulates wildly – so much, in fact, that every time I thought I had reached the summit, the road dropped away beneath me only to climb even further. At last I climbed the highest peak and got my first glimpse of the glittering bay, dotted with brightly coloured sails and dominated by the craggy fortress of Alcatraz. It's always funny to see something so famous in the flesh, as it were: like when you see the *Mona Lisa* for the first time, and realize that the print you had in your classroom was much bigger and clearer.

Alcatraz was up there with Colditz in my childhood imagination as the two worst places you could ever find yourself, should you break the law in some way. When I saw it there in the bay, it looked strangely peaceful, with its sandy-coloured buildings and quaint water tower. If it had been in London, someone would have turned it into a boutique hotel by now. I'm told that the name derives from the Spanish for 'Pelican Island', but I guess Al

Capone and its other famous inmates wouldn't have sounded so scary if they had gone there. ('So, where is Al being held, then?' 'Oh, he's gone to Pelican Island.')

So Alcatraz it is.

It wasn't very busy, so I walked down the hill towards Fisherman's Wharf, with its restaurants and gift shops stacked full of black-and-white striped aprons bearing slogans about 'the most dangerous cook in Alcatraz'. I saved my money. Near the wharf itself, people were standing around shellfish stalls, where the air was full of the sounds of chefs chopping and the cracking of crab shells. Steam billowed from dozens of open pots and the smell of clam and crab chowder filled my lungs. Men shouted in all directions, trying to get people into their restaurants, and the giant metal saucepans clattered more loudly than Prokofiev 2. I found a table in one of the crowded booths and sat warming up with a cup of clam chowder steaming gently in my hand and some spitting, sizzling crab cakes, the chilli stinging my lips, in the other. As I warmed up I could feel my eyelids drooping, so I set off again into the blustery, cold afternoon air to explore more of this wonderful city.

That evening, many of us were invited round to former LSO principal conductor Michael Tilson Thomas's beautiful house, where he fed us all with dim sum and some lovely wine. It was remarkable to see notes and pictures signed to 'MTT' by some of the great figures of 20th-century music: he had a little quote written to him by Stravinsky, something else from Diaghilev, and so many others, I can't remember them all. Best of all were two rather snazzy tailcoats in black and blue sequins which turned out to be some of James Brown's old stage clothes: the hardest-working man in showbiz (after Valery, of course). I can't tell you how much I wanted to try them on. I didn't, though. It was typical of Michael's generosity to open up his house to us

Michael Tilson Thomas rehearsing the LSO in Spain.

the day before he was leaving town himself, when I'm sure he had plenty of other things to do.

That was all yesterday. Today we had the first concert, an all-Prokofiev night. It was a bit tight as we rehearsed; there was only half an hour's break before the public came in, and the poor old piano tuner only had ten minutes to tune the piano. Fortunately we were doing the *Concerto for the Left Hand*, so it didn't take him as long as normal.

We started the show with the Classical Symphony, and the audience called Valery on three times afterwards. The piano soloist, Alexei Volodin, did an encore as well, using both hands, and they enjoyed it so much – despite the left-handed tuning, it sounded pretty good, too.

More stylish travel

At this moment in time, we are flying up the coast to San Diego, where we have a concert tonight before going on to Costa Mesa. It says on my schedule that this is a 'Ryanair-style flight'. I have no idea what this means. Perhaps some kind of upgraded, groovy charter for fashion designers and models? We, of course, would fit right in. Sadly, now that I am wedged firmly in my seat and have been shown the prices for the drinks and 'appetizing snacks', I fear I may have misunderstood the concept.

We each had numbers on our boarding passes, and had to line up next to the appropriately numbered poles. After standing around for half an hour, I got bored and went to get a coffee, which of course got the queue moving straight away. I leapt back into my allotted position, and when I got to the front of the queue the attendant called my number. I said, 'Bingo!' He was unimpressed.

'I'm just doing my job, sir. Please move along, or we may have to deplane.'

I have no idea what this means either.

We are leaving San Francisco, and I think I have left a little bit of my heart there. We had a great time: such warm and friendly people, and I have to admit to getting a thrill playing in Davies Symphony Hall.

The show this evening began with Prokofiev 2 – probably the loudest symphony in the universe, and at times unrelenting. I wasn't playing in that one, but could still hear it thundering through the walls for 35 minutes, by which time the audience had been pinned back into their seats. You could almost hear a collective sigh of relief as the pounding gave way to Beethoven's Piano Concerto No. 5 with Volodin. It was fascinating to hear him play such a different piece after his stunning playing the previous night, although this time he used both hands for the whole concerto.

By the time we went back on for the second half it was already 10 p.m.; jet lag was lurking despite the backstage coffee, which was the same viscosity as crude oil. But no matter how tired we all feel, Valery manages to whip up a storm. We played Prokofiev 7, one of my favourites: one of those pieces in which the sound of the band takes my breath away. The big tune starts off low and soars in a huge arc, which makes it completely orchestral, as the range it encompasses would take you from bass to soprano if you tried to sing it. But the wonderful thing about it is that it is played in three octaves at once, from the basses right up to Sharon's piccolo, and the sound is immense. Valery said in rehearsal that he thinks it sounds like a giant bird soaring over the mountains. He asked us to make as long a phrase as possible, and not to flap our wings too much. By the time the melody returns near the end of the last movement, it is at its grandest, and as I looked up in the concert Valery was conducting with a big smile on his face, arms outstretched like a giant bird. We knew just what he wanted, and I remembered the soaring birds over Alcatraz the day before. The audience roared their approval and we did a little encore.

It was some Prokofiev.

It has been 20 years since the LSO was last in San Francisco. I hope we don't leave it so long next time.

Chicago Black (and White) Sox

It's one of those days on tour when you'd quite like to be able to pop home for a bit. It's Mothering Sunday back in the UK; thanks to the webcam on my laptop, I was able not only to talk to my family, but to inspect the cuts and bruises from various rugby matches and bike accidents.

After speaking to my mum, I was reminded of the need for motherly care no matter how old you are. I had just got changed and come up the stairs in Chicago to see Tim Hugh, our principal cellist, fiddling with his socks. It was one of those horribly long days where we had to check out of our hotel before the concert, which meant making sure we had everything we needed for the rest of the day with us. Inevitably somebody forgets a bow tie or similar item, but usually a spare is found in time. This afternoon, Tim had forgotten his black socks. Given his position at the front of the orchestra, this is quite important, especially as the socks he had on were striped black and white ones.

The scene that met me at the top of the stairs was of Tim colouring in the white stripes on his socks with a black marker pen. They were thin stripes, and it was taking him ages. Just after he finished, someone suddenly found a spare pair of black socks. Maybe on future tours we should take a mum with us for moments like this.

The concert in Chicago was fantastic. Chicago Symphony Orchestra Hall is a wonderful venue with an incredible history, and the orchestra played out of its skin – especially as the Chicago Symphony had played the night before and we had something to prove. As the final notes of No. 5 flew out into the hall, the audience rose to their feet. Valery was smiling again, but this time it was after the Classical Symphony, so I relaxed.

There was no time to stop: we had a plane to catch. We were on the last flight out of Chicago, and I dozed off on the plane. When I woke up, New York was unfolding beneath us. It was nearly midnight, and the lights along the linear street patterns glowed bronze. The metropolitan area looked like an elaborate Christmas decoration made of copper, glistening in the winds below. Looking down at the city, my home for the next two days, I began to feel the excitement of a child staring at the tree with its twinkling lights. You never quite know what's going to happen.

That familiar journey through dull-looking suburbs never quite prepares me for the breathtaking sight of a floodlit Manhattan

Valery Gergiev and Andrew Haveron discuss a musical point in Chicago.

as you approach one of the bridges. When you first see it from the bus, everybody stops talking and just looks at it, almost pinching themselves to check that they are really there. In the middle of a long tour away from home, friends, family, and my mum, the sight of the skyscrapers glowing the way they do – just like in the movies – is very comforting.

Despite the fact that it changes every time we come here, it never really changes at all. It's noisy, smelly, exciting, and always welcomes us with open arms. It's good to be back.

Time to go home ... nearly

I love American audiences. When they enjoy a concert, they whoop and holler and stand up and shout, and it feels great. Since I last wrote, we've been to Boston, Washington DC, and Newark, and yesterday we arrived back in NYC for the final two concerts. We came in by bus, and this time the skyscrapers met the low grey clouds: it was eerie to see the tops of the buildings fading out above your head.

After a party hosted by the wonderful Jane Moss at the Lincoln Center last night, we were all a bit tired at this morning's rehearsal – especially Valery. As it was all repertoire we knew well, we played through some bits and pieces, mainly slowly, and then went for an early lunch. It felt a little like we had to get through the show and then we could go home: just a few more hours of concentration. Of course I hadn't bargained on one thing: Valery.

I don't know what he has for breakfast, but it must include at least twenty-five Shredded Wheat. When he flew onto the stage for the final concert, it quickly became clear that we were not going to go quietly into that good night. We were raging.

By the time we came back on for the second half and our final symphony of the cycle, Prokofiev 5, Valery looked like a man possessed. He drove us harder than ever and any tiredness

Nigel Thomas (timpani) rests before the concert in New York.

evaporated in a hot, sweaty, fever-pitched show. It's not often that we, bunch of cynics that we are, come offstage smiling and having had so much fun; but the concert tonight will remain in my memory for many years. If you were there, I doubt you will forget it. Every section of the band stood up to huge cheers from the audience. Nobody knows how to judge a concert quite like Valery.

We leave at 5.30 a.m., but I am writing this at 1 a.m. because I have to. We had to wind down with a drink after the concert; as we are in Manhattan, a cocktail was in order. I'll give you the recipe for my favourite.

One fiery Russian spirit

96 international Mixers

Seven dashes of Prokofiev

Four concertos

Three Solo players

Eight cities

13 concerts

Shake, stir, set alight, sit back, and enjoy.

I did.

New York City

'A'wight, boys and girls? Welcome to Landon Eafrow. I'm Dave, your driver, an' I only bin 'ere five minutes, so we might get lost – I 'ope you ain't nervous!'

This was the last straw on a very long trip to New York City.

We had been on a very cramped, hot plane for seven hours, and for some reason the JFK immigration people had decided to make the queuing process even more hideous than usual. We stepped off the plane and walked all of ten metres before joining a queue in a long corridor, with a very low ceiling, which remarkably managed to be even hotter than the plane. I tried to remain positive by imagining that this new system meant that once we got around the corner ahead, we would be through much more quickly.

In fact, this was an extra queue in advance of the normal queue. We stood for 90 minutes.

My fellow flute players Sharon and Siobhan were in front of me at the desk. When I went through, the lady asked me if I was in the symphony. I told her I was.

'And what do you play, sir?'

'I play the flute.'

'Really, that's nice. You don't look like a flute player.'

'Oh ... er ... thanks?' (Maybe Sharon and Shiv were the only flute players she had ever met.)

By the time we got through to the luggage rack, the belt had stopped moving and half the cases were stuck somewhere in the bowels of the machine, so we had to find someone to start it up again. The management sorted it out, as they always do, which left us to trudge across the road to the bus. This was where we met Dave, the driver.

As I've mentioned, a highlight of arriving here is the moment just before you go down into the tunnel to Manhattan: all of a sudden, in front of you is the beautiful panorama of New York in all its twinkling glory. Typically, at this point, the terrible plane food and immigration headaches disappear, and an enormous sense of expectation fills the body. This time, we had Dave.

I imagine his professional 'cockerney' routine goes down

well with Dick Van Dyke fans; however, as we had left London only a few hours earlier, this time his chirpy, well-rehearsed patter was met with a groan and a collective thought of 'Please make him stop.'

Dave realized this and did stop, thank goodness. His ex-Londoner qualities resurfaced, however, when we arrived at the hotel and one of the viola section tried to open the door to the luggage hold. Dave turned and snarled at him, whilst slamming the door shut again, 'Leave that door alone, it's my job.'

Whoa, easy, fella. I suppose in these uncertain times, he was just being protective of his job, but I was glad he picked a viola player to shout at, as they are used to it.

I blew away the cobwebs of the day by going for a run around Central Park, where I was impressed at the number of New Yorkers running up hills while maintaining conversations on their hands-free mobiles. It is slightly disconcerting to approach people in the middle of Central Park who appear to be talking to themselves; checking my GPS watch afterwards, I could see where my pace had quickened several times in an attempt to outrun these people. Soon, though, I grew used to seeing them running along talking and gesticulating in the air all on their own.

Later I went with friends to see the New York Knicks play the Boston Celtics at Madison Square Garden. I had never been to a basketball game before, and was surprised at how much entertainment was on offer: the game itself often seemed secondary to the time-out diversions of dancing girls (great), hoop-shooting for $1,000 competition (tricky), disco dancing (odd), and kids dressing up in full-size Knicks gear and then trying to run and score a basket (hilarious). We had to have foot-long hot dogs with knish and beer with a straw, and we joined in with all the shouting. If you ever come to the US and have a free evening, I can recommend it as a great American night out.

We have a rehearsal in an hour with Bernard, and I have my pass, which reads 'Gareth Davies – Great Performer'. I feel a little nervous, which makes me look a bit more like a flute player at last.

Central P... p... p... parky

We have a relatively short morning before catching the bus to Philadelphia. It looks sunny from my hotel room, but there is ice on the ground after yesterday morning's early snow flurries. The trees are frozen in white like a Christmas cake decoration, occasionally dropping some of their décor on unsuspecting passersby.

As I ventured across Columbus Circle towards Central Park earlier, the ferociousness of the cold hit me; despite having been running for a few minutes, my face and upper body were numb with cold. The neon sign that looks down on the circle read '7.45am; 17 degrees'. That is seventeen degrees Fahrenheit for those of you in the UK: cold. Unusually for New York, there weren't many other runners around. I quickened my pace and switched my iPod to shuffle.

Mahler 7. I didn't want to listen to that; I've got to play it tonight, and it is not one of my favourite pieces anyway, so I skipped ahead. Led Zeppelin. That was better: with Jimmy Page shredding, Robert Plant wailing, and the fact that I can't wait to get back into the warmth, I thought I might break my personal best on this route. My iPod has an eclectic mix of things on it: things I listen to for fun, things I think I should listen to but haven't got round to yet, and things that I am listening to because I have to play them soon, as well as a few bits and pieces that we have recorded in the LSO. As I am running and Led Zeppelin finish in a howl of feedback, a very quiet piece of

Chamber music in New York City – Gareth Davies, Sarah Quinn, Robert Turner and Alastair Blayden.

music starts, and it sounds familiar but I can't quite place it. As the music gets louder I realize that it is a soundtrack for a film we recorded a few years ago with Alexandre Desplat, which starred Nicole Kidman; it was called *Birth*.

It starts with four flutes playing a rhythmic pattern, with a very sparse accompaniment of triangle and pizzicato strings, and this repetitive pattern builds up. I remember it very well, as I had to play all four parts one after the other in a session that started at 10 p.m. in Abbey Road the day after my daughter was born. Running round Central Park, I was in fact listening to four of me. The opening scene from the film, which is where this piece of music comes from, is a long shot of a man running around Central Park. There is no ambient noise in the shot, just the music.

It was only as the music reached a crescendo, just as I ran

under a stone bridge in the middle of the park, that I remembered that at this point in the film the runner stopped running, put his hands to his chest, had a heart attack, and died. I flicked back to Mahler 7, and made my way back to the hotel to thaw out.

Have a nice day

It's not uncommon now to see a little bit of American culture creeping into daily life in London. You know the kind of thing: the coffee chains, the way people inflect the end of sentences to make it sound like a question? But every time I come here, I'm reminded that while it may be similar in some ways, it's different in a whole lot of others – different in a good way.

The boys from the Berlin Phil are in London this week with Sir Simon Rattle, and when they arrived at the Barbican they will have found it just as we left it. When we arrived yesterday at the highly impressive Kimmel Center in Philadelphia, we went upstairs and found an enormous players' lounge with a dartboard, chess, and other games, and extremely comfy sofas to fall asleep on. There was a lady in the corner with tea, coffee, and fruit for the orchestra, guarding a huge cake that read 'Welcome London Symphony Orchestra' – a gift from the Philadelphia Orchestra. Isn't that nice? We didn't even leave a muffin for Berlin. I feel a bit guilty, but that's the USA for you. I hope someone will let them know how grateful we all were. The hall itself is magnificent for orchestra and audience alike, and Mahler 7 was dispatched in typical Gergiev style. Sadly, there was no time to enjoy the sights of the city, but I really hope to be back, as part of my running regime in foreign places really does need to take in the run up the steps to the Museum of Art; or, as the tour guide I spoke to called them, the Rocky Steps.

We arrived back in NYC very late, and today we repeat

Mahler 7 at the Lincoln Center, but not until we have done some sightseeing and shopping. In Japan, as I've mentioned before, there is a little ritual of shop assistants shouting when a customer enters: you aren't expected to respond, I think. The London equivalent is that you walk in and try to buy something, but the assistant is on the phone, or simply too cool to speak to you. Funnily enough, in New York, there are also rules of engagement in shops: whenever you walk in, someone asks how you are doing. I always respond by saying that I'm fine, even if I'm not: it's the British way. If I ask how they are, they either look confused or don't answer. I stare at the floor and shuffle off as they continue asking other people how they are. After walking for miles around the city I decided to stop for a coffee. I find my accent seems to confuse people, especially if I say 'Please may I have ...' instead of 'Can I get ...'. Despite this, as with the Philadelphia Orchestra, they like to go the extra mile here.

'Hi. How are you today? What can I get for you?'

'Hi. I'm fine thank you. How are...oh, never mind. Please may I have a small black coffee?'

'OK. So that's a tall Americano.'

'Yes, please.'

'And what is your name?'

'I'm sorry?'

'What is your name?'

'Oh ... er ... Gareth.'

'Garry?'

'No, Gareth.'

'Garret?'

'Gareth. Ga-reth.'

'OK.' (*to another server*) 'Tall Americano for Gareth.'

'Garret?'

'No, Ga-reth.'

I waited, and was presented with a cup of coffee with my name written on it.

'There you go, Garry. Have a good day.'

I tried an experiment this morning in a different branch. I ordered the same thing.

'So that's a tall Americano. Great, and what's your name sir?'

'My name? My name is, er ... Valery.'

'Tall Americano for Valery.'

I quickly received my coffee, with 'Valery' written on the cup. There was no queue behind me. Gergiev opens doors around here.

'You have a great day, Valery.'

In the city that never sleeps, it's impossible not to have a great day, whatever your name is.

I had a nice day, but it's time to go home

The snow in New York City has now melted, and been replaced by rain. I seem to spend entire afternoons being hit by massive raindrops falling from canopies on the front of buildings. Still, it makes a change from lumps of snow.

Today was our final show before returning home: Mahler 9 and 10 (the Adagio). Most of the orchestra went for one last enormous American breakfast before heading down to the Lincoln Center for the rehearsal. As it was a Sunday morning, all of New York was out enjoying the sunshine that had at last broken through the cloud. The rehearsal had an invited audience made up of friends of the Lincoln Center and some friends of the LSO: there must have been about 300 people there. Valery rehearsed Mahler 10 quite a lot, and then did some bits and bobs on 9. We reached the final movement, which he didn't want to play just before the show. After the incredible string opening (the LSO strings sounding wonderful) there is a passage for wind. I was asked to play *pp* in the top register, something which is never easy after the exertions of the third movement. Valery stopped.

'Woodwind, a little more expressive, don't play so quietly in this hall.'

We tried again. He stopped.

'Still a little louder. I know it says *pp* but in this acoustic it is too quiet. It should sound expressive.'

He looked around nervously and wrapped his arms around himself, 'It shouldn't sound like you are playing with no clothes on. You know what I mean?'

We did. After the amount of food I've eaten this week, it wasn't a pleasant thought.

'It is at the end when it is very quiet and it slows down to just the violas' notes, that is when it should sound like it is on a life-support machine.'

Poor violas.

The rehearsal ended with applause from the audience. We waved – bowing was too formal – and left the stage to have something to eat again and get ready for the concert.

We have played Mahler 9 together many times. It is a piece that comes alive only in performance. The finale is so emotionally draining that you simply can't play it as a performance in every rehearsal: it's too much. You have to hold something back for the show. As Valery swooped onto the stage, the players could feel the anticipation. He waited for silence, looked up and brought the first murmur of sound out from the cellos and horn, barely audible until a few bars in, where the string section enters as a whole. The whole of this movement is so forward-looking musically, it is easy to forget how old it is. Valery seemed to search, trying to find a resting place through the tempo fluctuations, until the music eventually disappeared somewhere in the back of the hall. For the first time this week, nobody clapped between the movements. After the third movement, which is marked Rondo-Burlesque, there was an audible gasp from the audience and a lady near the front whispered very loudly, 'Wow!' Valery looked down and smiled. Unusually for him, he paused before the final movement and stood motionless, waiting for silence, before diving into the finale, sculpting the music with every finger. The string section played with almost unbearable intensity near the end of the piece, helped by the acoustic; as the music died away, it wasn't long before half of the audience erupted, whilst the rest sat slightly stunned and eventually rose to their feet. It was a great show.

We had a short time before we had to go back to the hotel and then the airport. I chanced it one more time and returned to the coffee shop. In order to appreciate fully the subtlety of what happened next, you'll need to read the next section with a New Yorker accent.

Valery Gergiev – it needs to be a bit more like this.

'Tall Americano, please.'

'Sure, and your name please, sir?'

'My name? My name is Valery.' The woman next to me in the queue did a double take.

'One tall Americano for Larry!' shouted the server. I went to collect my coffee. 'Here's your coffee, Larry. Have a nice day.'

Time to go home.

A history lesson

'Black Americano for Colin, please.'

Killing fifteen minutes before my appointment, I ventured into a coffee chain. Jet lag had temporarily severed the connection between my brain and my mouth. I couldn't face the look of confusion on the face of the barista when confronted with my name, and so blurted out the first name that popped into my head: Colin. I considered saying Sir Colin, but thought better of it: it would be even less likely than Valery.

I stood at the end of the row with that strange feeling that the earth was shifting under my feet, and waited. It took me a while to realize that the man at the end had called out my 'name' several times. If I was going to play this game, I'd have to be awake.

I perched on a stool looking out across Broadway. It was raining heavily, and the wind funnelling down the road was pushing it sideways. A bin outside was spilling out skeletal umbrellas, like fossilized bird wings. I cupped my hands around the coffee and steamed gently. I had an appointment across the road at the Carnegie Hall Archive, where they have an enormous amount of material going back to the opening of the hall in 1891. Rob, one of the archivists, had agreed to show me some material from the time of the LSO's 1912 visit.

At the appointed time I showed my photo ID and went up to the nineteenth floor, where I was greeted by huge posters of a grinning Michael Tilson Thomas and various other famous musicians. I walked down the long corridor towards a man at a desk. He looked rather surprised at being approached.

'Hello, sir, may I help you?'

'Hello, yes, I have an appointment to see Rob Hudson at two o'clock.'

He looked at me. I was a little bedraggled: wet clothes, hair stuck to my head, and a faraway look in my eyes. He narrowed his eyes.

'Who?'

'Er ... Rob Hudson? At two? The archivist?'

He folded his arms and gave me a Paddington Bear stare.

'Rock Hudson? We don't have a Rock Hudson.' He clearly thought I was wasting his time and had somehow got past security on a flaky excuse for star-spotting.

'No, not Rock Hudson; he is no longer with us, I believe. No, *Rob* Hudson.' I smiled. A lot.

'Oh, Rob Hudson the archivist?'

'Er, yes.'

The suspicious look passed as he called Rob and asked me to take a seat. I spent the next hour talking to Rob and looking at century-old documents, which he kindly agreed to scan for me. He told me about the history of the place, and we discussed the tour of 1912, for which he had the original Carnegie Hall programme. It was like going back in time. One flyer caught my eye, as it had a Union Jack on it. It was from a concert in 1960 with the LSO, and on the back was a picture of the conductors: Pierre Monteux, the main conductor, who was 85 at the time, and on his right, a younger guest conductor by the name of Colin Davis.

At the Lincoln Center later that day, Sir Colin Davis was sitting backstage talking to players before the rehearsal. Such is the affection for this great man in the LSO that nobody walks past him without stopping to talk, and he doesn't appear to mind one bit. To top it all, Nikolaj Znaider was playing the Sibelius Violin Concerto. It has been well documented how much influence Colin has had on him, and to see the two of them together was a wonderful thing. As I sat on the stage and thought about how long he has been conducting us, the people he has worked with, and the link with the musical past that he is, I felt a strange sense of historical weight. We all know that Colin is slower when he walks on now, and has to sit down for the shows, being a similar age to Monteux back in that 1960s concert; but when I am his age, I don't think anyone will want to listen to my flute playing. Besides, I'll be too busy watching *Countdown*.

At the concert, Nikolaj led them out to applause and Colin followed cautiously behind. As Colin appeared at the front,

The author talks to Gino Francesconi, director of the Carnegie Hall Archive.

the sudden increase in intensity of clapping would have made a passer-by assume we had already played: it seemed that New Yorkers were pleased to see him. Colin sculpted the opening line from the strings and the solo line wove in and out, the soloist and conductor doing what they do best. Colin couldn't resist standing up from his chair as he whipped his baton down in that familiar sideswipe which brings a deep rumble from the lower end of the orchestra in this massive hall. He sat down again, looked across at me and raised his eyebrows with a twinkle in his eye, as if he knew somebody was going to tell him off later for standing, but couldn't help himself.

After the concerto was finished, Nikolaj came back on and spoke. 'I don't know if it's the done thing to play an encore here ...'

The audience erupted in whoops and cheers.

He then dedicated his stunning performance of Bach to Sir Colin. The room was spellbound until the last note faded away.

♩ ♩ ♩

The door opened to let Nikolaj go offstage. I looked to the side, and sitting on the small chair in the wings was Colin, listening and waiting. Nikolaj embraced him and the two of them sat together and carried on talking as we all filed past, shaking hands and patting backs. Unforgettable.

Shopping in the dark just isn't cool

There are many things in New York I would like to share with my family. It doesn't seem right going up the Empire State Building on my own; sadly, half-term is the week after the tour ends. Before the concert, desperately trying to find presents for everyone, I found myself lurking outside an intimidating shop that seemed to cater for the very young, thin, and beautiful – categories that do not apply to me. Music blared from within, even though it was 10 a.m., and the lights were so low I could not see what it actually sold. However, I had to venture inside, as I had orders from home. The shop was called Hollister.

I eventually plucked up the courage to go in. It reminded me of an art installation I once visited at Tate Modern, where you walked into a pitch-black room designed to make you more aware of senses other than sight. This shop took it one step further in that, as well as the almost total darkness, your aural abilities were impaired by the ear-splitting music. The three bulbs they had installed all seemed to be pointed directly at my eyes, rendering me temporarily blind. I was looking for T-shirts for my boys. There were hundreds of them, but it was so dark, they might all have been the same colour. Or not. I started to sweat, and a young man wearing one of the T-shirts came over.

'Hey, buddy!'

'Er ... hey!'

My boys would be crushed with embarrassment, but at least he didn't ask me how I was. However, that was the end of our conversation. I walked around, and every so often a young man or woman wearing hardly anything popped out from behind a plant and said, 'Hey, buddy!' I don't know where they get these people from, but they are all unbelievably perfect specimens. Not very good at small talk, mind. Ten minutes later, I was still wandering around squinting in the darkness, my face etched with pain from the decibel level. I simply couldn't see what I was looking at: a red T-shirt or a green one? A young lady came and stood next to me.

'Hey, buddy!'

'Oh ... er ... hey!'

'Do you need some help?'

'Actually, yes, I do. I can't see what colour the T-shirts are.'

She laughed and said, 'For sure, a lot of people your age say that.'

Before I could feel irritated, she smiled the biggest smile I have ever seen, with the whitest teeth imaginable. For about five seconds, the glow of her teeth lit up the racks of T-shirts. I grabbed a red one and a green one before she stopped smiling and the light went out once more. As quickly as possible, I paid and left.

In my haste to leave the shop, I almost bumped into three women. They smiled, slightly less impressively.

'Excuse me, are you from Noo York?'

'I'm afraid not! I'm from London.'

The three of them turned and looked at one another.

'Oh my gawd. Did you hear his accent?'

'I did! Oh my gawd, I looooove that Briddish accent.'

'Oh, wow, me too. Say, you know who you sound like?'

'I really have no idea.'

'He does, doesn't he?'

'Yes! Yes, he does!'

'You know, you sound just like Hugh Grant.'

'Yes, you do. Hugh Grayant.'

'We love Hugh Grant!'

'We love your Briddish accent!'

'Golly, really. Wow, gosh, thanks. You, erm ... have a good day, ladies.'

It was 10.30 a.m., and I had been forced into a parody of myself. I felt very uncool indeed, although I confess that this did have something to do with it being my 40th birthday last week. There. I've said it out loud. After my stressful experience in the shop, I realized I was actually rather looking forward to playing *Missa Solemnis* with Sir Colin that evening. The piece had really grown on me, and it is also easier to play at Lincoln Center than it had been at the Albert Hall back in the summer (despite the fact that I was still in my thirties then).

We started the rehearsal with the opening chords, and Colin looked and listened. The balance was pretty good, and after about ten minutes he called the rehearsal to a halt.

'Really, I think we should stop. Let's leave it until the concert.'

And so we finished early, which gave everyone a chance to have a cup of tea. As I walked off stage, Colin approached.

'Mr Davies. I owe you an apology.'

'Really, Sir Colin? Whatever for?'

'For not using all of the rehearsal.'

'I don't see many angry faces around, do you?'

He gave me one of his cheeky smiles, 'No! Quite!' He disappeared into the lift.

An hour or so later we all reassembled on the stage with the magnificent LSO Chorus behind us. Colin walked on with the soloists, and we began. There are times when this piece feels like it goes on for ever, but not that night; in fact, I enjoyed it so much, I almost wished it *could* go on for ever. The reviews of the concert tried, but failed, to pinpoint exactly why it was so good: something Colin does, or something in the way he is, gets right to the heart of the work. The orchestra has enormous affection for Colin; but the way the chorus sang for him proved that we aren't the only ones. They were truly breathtaking.

Earlier that day I had been half listening to the TV, and the story on the local news was that *GQ* magazine had announced that Brooklyn – specifically Williamsburg – was the coolest place on the planet. This had obviously upset some people, mainly people in Manhattan who disagreed, and also people in Brooklyn who didn't really want everyone coming in and spoiling it. After a day when I had been too uncool to find the correct T-shirt, and then reminded some women of Hugh Grant, it then came as a relief to perform in a concert that was way beyond cool. Who needs to worry about being cool when you get to work with Colin in NYC, in a performance like that?

Sharon grabbed me immediately after the show.

'Come on, we're going out to celebrate your birthday!'

In secret, she had organized about 20 people to meet us. I was touched.

'So where are we going?' I asked.

'It's a little restaurant I found. It's really cool!'

'Great, where is it?' I asked as we descended into the subway.

'We have to get on the train because it's in Williamsburg, in Brooklyn.'

I smiled. 'Did you see the thing about *GQ* on the news today, then?'

'No, what was that?'

'Oh, nothing. Let's go.'

Sharon just *is* cool.

IO A Party in Boston?
1912

A cocktail of overconfidence and historical tension meant that things were never going to be easy in Boston. Whether it was the memory of the Boston Tea Party lingering in the collective consciousness of the critics, or an instinctive resistance to the LSO's claim to be the greatest orchestra in the world, we shall never know; but the critical reception was not good. In fact, it was downright vicious.

When the players arrived after a train journey of over six hours in which Nisbet complained of seeing absolutely 'no vegetation the whole journey', it was snowing. Turner was impressed: 'Boston looks like a homely English town. I like it up to now. Much better than New York.' Nisbet was less impressed and said that the town was 'not unlike Glasgow', although he did admit that, as it was snowing, he hadn't been able to see much.

That polarity of opinion was mirrored by the views Bostonians took of the orchestra. The balcony was nearly full for the concert, largely because of the appearance of the former principal conductor of the BSO; the *Boston Daily Globe* headline was 'Nikisch Returns!' However, the stalls hadn't sold very well, perhaps because the cost of the whole tour was such that ticket prices were high. The *Globe* did acknowledge that

> Such a conductor deserved a hearing which would have taxed the capacity of the house. There was great enthusiasm nevertheless after all the numbers, occasioning Mr Nikisch and his players to make repeated acknowledgement. It should be the source of general pleasure that the distinguished conductor will give another concert at Symphony Hall.

The audience enjoyed the programme greatly, calling the conductor and orchestra to take many bows. However, enjoyment and musical integrity in the eyes of the music critic are not easy bedfellows, and the rest of the review ripped the orchestra to shreds. Fairly predictably, the much-missed hero Nikisch was praised in measures equal to the scorn heaped upon the LSO. It can be summed up in the headline from that evening's review: 'Nikisch Conducts. Readings Again Disclose Poetic Beauty. Inferiority of London Orchestra Apparent.'

The reviews of the concerts in Boston in 1912 were only a little shy of a demolition of the entire orchestra and an affirmation of the supremacy of the local band. They are some of the worst reviews I have ever read in my entire life. The *Boston Daily Globe* said, 'The magnitude of Nikisch as an interpretative conductor of sensibility and imagination and authority, is conceded by all, yet why should a large public pay $3 to hear him play upon not only a mediocre but an inferior instrument?'

The rest of the review is founded upon this principle: that Nikisch is wonderful, but the orchestra is bad, which is why it didn't sound very good. It points out that the ragged edges in tone, quality, and precision simply wouldn't happen in the

Boston Symphony Orchestra, and gleefully celebrates the departure of the young upstarts from London:

> The respectable members of this visiting organization have now departed to become again the chief pillars in the temple of British art. We congratulate their patrons for every occasion upon which they sit under the inspired ministrations of Mr Nikisch and we also commiserate them upon such an orchestra as this as their best exponent of symphonic art.

As the players travelled around the country, they often did catch glimpses of the reviews, but in general were fed little bits and pieces by the management (mainly the good bits). But the review in Boston seems to have filtered through. Turner remarks on it in his diary:

> I got another good word. A paper says I am a performer of the highest rank. Note the difference in opinions in the critics. Many of them are very ignorant and write quite rudely and uneducated and they are full of the Almighty Boston Symphony Orchestra. I would like to hear it. Nearly all Germans. Impartial people and musicians like us better, but the papers, No.

In 1912, despite the fame of the Boston orchestra, Turner had never actually heard them, and one can sense his irritation that although they must be good, of course, this was mainly down to the presence of imported foreigners. Not long before, they had been almost exclusively an orchestra of Germans, even conducting rehearsals in German! In the years to come, as the recording of orchestras became commonplace, the distinctive sound of both bands would be heard all over the world. Unfortunately for the LSO, the critics in Boston had the benefit of hearing both outfits, and the comparisons became more and more personal. Not content with sneering rather unkindly about the orchestra as a whole, the *Globe*'s reviewer gradually became more precise in his criticism, focusing in on sections and then on individual players. He reported that the string section was lacking in uniformity and precision, and that the double-bass section in particular was habitually late. He summed up their performance thus: 'From a position at a kindly distance the combined strings give a hale and hearty tone in fortissimo as becomes them; they do not invite microscopic observation.'

However upset the string players might have been about his opinions, the unfortunate woodwind players were singled out for a special kind of vitriol ('Then there came members of the woodwind section, which gave forth strange and uncertain sounds'). He then proceeded to admit that the principal clarinettist, Manuel Gomez, was an artist, but played sharp nonetheless, and used a reed that gave him a sound which was 'neither fish nor flesh'. George Ackroyd, principal flute, was said to make a good sound even though he used a wooden instrument, although he couldn't articulate at all. Principal oboe William Malsch was given a paragraph all of his own:

> The piping and virginal modesty of the oboe's tone already has been duly celebrated. After listening to the incomparable art of Mr Longy [the French-born principal oboe of the Boston Symphony Orchestra], it is not particularly enlivening to hear the passages in Tchaikovsky's noble and much maltreated symphony or those in the 'Tristan' prelude proceeding from what might be a child's toy rather than a musical instrument. This is verily the worst oboe playing heard along this shore since the advent of the so-called Dresden Symphony Orchestra, whose oboist might have been the ship's cook, who had acquired the skill en route.

Once again, Nikisch was singled out for his poetic ability with music, and the LSO got the blame for the poor execution of his artistic ideas:

> The pity then of witnessing a conductor of Mr Nikisch's caliber playing upon an organization which is deplorably delinquent,

yet has been called the 'best orchestra in the world'. The ambition to disclose to the new world what the program – again for the consideration of a quarter – affirms to be 'the highest possible musical offering that the Old world can send us' is a noble one – although there are orchestras in Berlin, Vienna and Paris to be pondered upon for the moment – yet curiosity aside, it would have been quite as acceptable to have brought Mr Nikisch to America to [play with] orchestras with less royal patronage but more musical distinction.

There is no record of what the orchestra thought, or indeed the reaction of Busby or Pew, but there must have been a sense that their meticulous plans were gradually unravelling. Pew might have been beginning to wonder whether he had made a terrible miscalculation in booking the orchestra. Also, the King's patronage, which had been so useful in securing Fales's sponsorship, seemed now to be working against them. The press had seen the letter from the King, and were unimpressed. They had read the programme (which they had had to pay for) and seen the extravagant claims. They had sat back in their chairs and waited to be impressed; or maybe there was nothing the LSO could have done to impress them. Whatever the reasons, the first impression made by the orchestra was only lukewarm in New York, and in Boston the critics dropped its reputation right to the bottom of the harbour.

Whether it was the dressing-down from the critics, or just that it took the orchestra a while to settle into their stride, once the LSO had left Boston they approached the tour with a renewed vigour. Now they really did have something to prove.

II The Universal Language of Mankind
2012

Method music

You may be familiar with the theory behind method acting. Roughly speaking – and I'm no expert – rather than simply imagining yourself as a criminal gangster while acting in a film, you actually rob a bank as part of your research and stay in character throughout the duration of filming. Or something like that, anyway. Robert De Niro famously trained as a boxer for his role in *Raging Bull* and gained the appropriate physique and associated skills: a landmark in method acting. For his role in *Taxi Driver*, which I have not seen, I imagine he did a fair amount of mini-cabbing around Brooklyn. Back to that later.

In 21st-century classical music, it's no longer enough simply to do concerts: an overture, a concerto, a symphony plus interval drinks. Now we all have to have marketing to keep up with other, more fashionable art forms. I don't think that this is a bad thing – it's a busy world out there with lots of distractions, and if you are passionate about something and want to tell people, then you have to shout about it. It's not a new idea, but we often have themes, like many other arts organizations, although of course we have always had concert series devoted to the works of one composer. Over the last few seasons we have had Mahler with Valery, and Beethoven with Haitink. One of the recent campaigns was the Emigré series, in which we programmed works of composers who had left their homelands for foreign lands. It was a fascinating evening, with the Stravinsky Symphony in 3 movements and the Schoenberg Violin Concerto played magnificently by Nikolaj Zneider. The second half of the concert was Rachmaninov's *Symphonic Dances*. I interviewed Valery the other day about the Emigré series, and about the way leaving your homeland can affect you. The three composers had very different experiences and different reasons for leaving their respective countries, although all of them ended up living fairly close to one another in Hollywood. Rachmaninov had left a pre-revolutionary Russia, whilst Stravinsky had left a rather different homeland, and you can clearly hear the difference in the pieces.

We played last night in Belgrade; not as part of the Emigré series, but the Rachmaninov was played, along with Prokofiev 5. Although Prokofiev wasn't an émigré, he travelled widely – at least until his passport wasn't renewed. Musicians as a whole seem to travel more and more these days. Digital technology still can't replicate the live experience, and long may that continue, although it does mean we are away from home a lot. As my long-suffering, patient and beautiful wife pointed out while I unpacked one case and packed another, I have spent more time out of the country than in it in the last two months: which is where we return to method acting, or in our case method music. What better ensemble could you ask for to play the music of émigrés, than an orchestra made up of people from every corner of the globe who spend a huge amount of time away from home? Music can make you feel a lot of things, but when you play those searing, bittersweet lines of Prokofiev and Rachmaninov on tour, and you long to be at home with your family, they take on an extra depth. It's hard on us, but quite something for you.

When I spoke to Valery, I asked him if he thought that Rachmaninov had an idealistic vision of an old Russia that no longer existed – a Russia that he saw through rose-tinted, rather than red-tinted spectacles – and did he think that this came through in *his* music? Did he think that Stravinsky had a more realistic view, because of his different experience in Russia, and did this come through in *his* music? Valery paused and thought for a while, so I then expanded my theory. I explained that my father left a small mining village in Wales in the 1960s. There wasn't really any work, the mines were closing, and so he moved to England. I often wonder when he expresses a fleeting thought that one day he might move back home, whether he would be

Alastair Blayden (cello) makes the long walk to the plane.

disappointed to find a very different place from the nostalgic, Dylan Thomas Wales of his childhood. I wonder whether he has an idealized view of a past that is no longer there. Did Valery think that this concept was similar to the experience his Russian émigré composers had been through?

Valery paused again and then roared with laughter. I waited for him to explain.

'I love that you compare the suffering of the Russian émigré composers with your father having to move from Wales to live in England! That is so funny!'

I thought about it, and realized how stupid I had been.

Rachmaninov had it easy.

La Dolce Vita

La Scala: the scene of so many operatic triumphs and disasters. I remember being told about it by my dad when I was a kid. We were listening to Maria Callas and Tito Gobbi (surely one of the greatest ever names for a singer); at the time, I would probably rather have been listening to Showaddywaddy or something of the sort, but I loved hearing tales about opera audiences booing bad singers and sometimes even throwing rotten tomatoes at them. I've never seen any rotten fruit for sale outside the opera on our visits, though, and so far, we haven't been troubled by any projectiles.

La Scala is beautiful both inside and outside. Although the sound is quite dry (not uncommon in opera houses), this does give it clarity. Backstage, in the cavernous space behind the flats, layer upon layer of curtains and backdrops are hoisted unbelievably high overhead. It is a very functional, dark area, and doesn't prepare you for the extravagant stage. If I were a Hollywood film director and wanted to film in an opera house that everyone would recognize as such, I would film here. It is what a child might draw, if asked to draw an old theatre.

The stage itself is made from plain, black-painted wooden boards, but raise your eyes up and you find a concoction as elaborate as a wedding cake. There is a circle of chairs on the flat in front of the stage, and rising up from the floor are several rows of balconies, each upholstered in red velvet with lamps on the wall. The hall itself is in the shape of a circle rather than a rectangle, allowing everyone in the audience an equally good view of the stage and the other concertgoers, which is at least 50 per cent of the reason for going.

After our rehearsal the hall filled up, and as we wandered off stage chatting, we nearly stumbled into a live television interview with principal guest conductor Daniel Harding chatting away in Italian. The producer put his finger to his lips, glared and pointed down to tell us to walk on tiptoe. It's a shame she didn't tell the audience to make less noise during the concert, but you can't have everything. It's funny how, despite the language and cultural differences around the world, all audiences have the same mobile ringtones.

Sitting waiting for the concert to begin, I looked around the hall. As in every Italian city I have played in, they were all dressed to the nines. Men in sharp suits stood talking at the back of the boxes, beautiful women draped themselves over the velvet balconies sipping champagne – it looked like a Versace photo shoot, and the beauty of the building was given a run for its money by the clientele. I felt scruffy, and I was wearing evening tails. Our bass clarinet player Lorenzo was clearly enjoying being back in his homeland, gesticulating even more than usual; he seemed to know everybody.

Mahler 6 in this compact space was intense, to say the least. After the final crushing blow of the symphony, there was a moment's silence until Daniel brought his arms down and the audience erupted. This piece is almost as much work to listen to as it is to play, but they appeared to have enjoyed their job. They cheered and looked beautiful, looking at each other, and then I heard more things that happen only in Italy; huge cheers of '*Bravi!*' and then when horn player Dave Pyatt takes a solo bow, '*Bravo!*' and principal bassoon Rachel Gough, '*Brava!*'

La Scala: beautiful hall, beautiful music, beautiful people, beautiful grammar ... and no tomatoes.

A long time ago, in a galaxy far, far away ...

After a couple of concerts in Shanghai we flew to Wuhan, a huge city on the banks of the Yangtze river. The airport is absolutely huge, with row upon row of empty stands for the planes. It is quite modern and looks like a super-Stansted, so it was with some bemusement that we descended the steps to find we were parked by the perimeter fence, a ten-minute bus ride from the terminal.

As we travelled through the city, the scale of development was quite overwhelming. Everywhere you looked, buildings were being ripped down and replaced with massive new structures of glass and steel. There seems to me to be no better picture to describe the birth of the new China from the old than the sight of a sleek, silver shard of glass at the top of a new apartment building that dwarfs everything around it. As you follow the building down from the sky, the builders are still taking the bamboo scaffolding and hessian covering down. It looks like a shiny new animal emerging from a 100-year-old cocoon.

I still feel as if I'm on an alien planet: everything is bigger and faster, and although the country is famed for its bicycles, there are probably more on the streets of London these days. Wuhan is full of luxury European-brand cars and old cabs which are having their last ounce of life squeezed out of them by drivers eager to impress. Our hotel is very new, as is the concert hall; in fact, we are the first international orchestra to visit.

Next door to the hotel is a huge tower of restaurants. Unlike when we came to China for the first time six years ago, many of them are Western chains. It seemed a shame to come all this way only to eat the worst of what we could have back home, so Chris Richards (principal clarinet), Joost Bosdijk (second bassoon) and I opted for lunch at the Chinese restaurant close by; we were quickly followed by half the band. Judging by the way people stared at us, they were not accustomed to huge groups of hungry Westerners suddenly turning up and pointing. Fortunately for us, the menu had pictures and English translations.

I was contemplating what kind of texture fried chilli chicken gizzard would have, or whether to have the congealed pig-blood pancake with chicken feet, when I spotted something that baffled me completely: as a starter, roasted papaya with wood bull-frog fallopian tubes. I hate roasted papaya, so decided on Sichuan chicken with rice. It did make me think, as I watched the man at the next table sucking some bird's head, that perhaps we British have become a little prudish about what parts of animals we eat. This time, though, I was content to be small-minded, marvel at the sheer culinary dexterity of the chef who dissects the wood bullfrogs, and hope I wouldn't meet him down a dark alley.

The concert hall is very impressive, full of enough gold to make Vienna's Musikverein look drab, and the sound is good too – so good, in fact, that our rehearsal was unbearably loud. We all hoped that with an audience in it, it would be a little quieter. My previous experience of audiences in China is that the clapping is sustained but polite; they don't whoop and holler in appreciation, and if the conductor wants to keep going on and off stage to milk the applause at the end, there is a risk that they'll simply leave. However, I hadn't banked on conductor Kristjan Järvi.

The audience seemed fascinated by this good-looking young man with long hair, who dances on the podium in front of the orchestra during *West Side Story*. I suppose he probably wasn't what they were expecting. To make things even better, the soloist, Jian Wang, is very well known here. Before he played a note on his cello, the audience was cheering. There was a roar as we finished the Shostakovich concerto; he came back on to play some Bach, and then again to play a Chinese song. You could hear the sound of people humming along, and the atmosphere in the hall was fantastic.

We returned after the interval and gave an uplifting performance of the *Symphonic Dances* by Rachmaninov. It was a huge workout for the orchestra, and Kristjan really drove the tempo, which drew an enormous effort from everyone on stage. As we raced to the final bars, the crowd was already clapping; when

Chi takes a bow in China.

we finished, they called Kristjan back on several times before we played a dance from *The Snow Maiden* by Tchaikovsky. Six million notes later, he came back on again, and the horns cried out the opening call of a piece called *Good News from Beijing*. There was a cheer as they recognized it, and as soon as the main melody started, the whole audience was clapping along. This wasn't something I'd seen before in China, and you could sense the whole band stepping up a gear despite being exhausted. The cheering at the end was deafening, and most people were on their feet shouting for more.

I looked around, and everybody on stage was smiling. It's always gratifying to get such a good reaction and see people enjoying what we do. Also, we knew what was coming next. Kristjan came on and faced us, the audience sat down, he brought his baton crashing down, and the unmistakable sound of the main title to *Star Wars* rang out. The audience went nuts (well, it looked that way, but to be honest we were making so much noise that I could just see a lot of movement). It is a piece we have been associated with for 30 years, and that trumpet sound, so closely linked with Maurice Murphy, is now in the safe hands of Philip Cobb. I had played the piece with many different orchestras over the years, but whenever we play it in the LSO (and we don't very often), it just sounds better. As the roaring continued through the final triumphant chord, everybody in the room was smiling. Kristjan had to drag us off the platform. What a great night.

We reconvened in the Bernstein Bistro (I'm sure he'd be delighted) for a few beers and discussed the show. It was a new place, not very efficient yet, and the beers took a while to arrive. When they finally did, they turned out to be alcohol-free and not terribly nice, so we ordered some draft. It ran out. We had just decided to try somewhere else, as we were officially thirsty, when Jian Wang appeared from upstairs carrying some bottles of beer. We had noticed lots of food and drink going upstairs, but hadn't realized he was up there.

'Do you want these beers? We ordered them but don't want them any more.'

'Thanks, Maestro, you have no idea how grateful we are. You are now my favourite cellist.'

He laughed, and left, clutching a cello over his shoulder and a plastic bag containing chickens' feet and ducks' jaws.

China: not just another country, but a whole other galaxy.

Universal language of the alien culture

Before our leaders began to *cut, cut, cut,* the repetitive phrase most familiar to British voters was *education, education, education.* We haven't forgotten that at LSO Towers, and this trip to China has seen us build on one of our players' great strengths: educational work with young people, or as we like to call it, Discovery. The name is fitting as, in my experience, it's a voyage of discovery, not only for the participants but for the players themselves. Whatever your ideas and plans for a day's visit to a school in Tower Hamlets, by the end of the day you will have gone to places you hadn't expected to go, heard sounds you couldn't possibly have anticipated, and seen a thousand smiles. You will be drained and exhilarated in equal measure.

It's one thing working with English-speaking kids in London, but some of our intrepid players flew out to Shanghai a day early to work with some schoolchildren there. By the time the rest of the orchestra arrived, they had completed a busy day of workshops. Chi speaks Chinese but, as far as I know, second violin Belinda McFarlane and bass trombone Paul Milner don't; and I haven't been made aware of a Dutch quarter in Shanghai, so I presume that Joost was also dependent on James Richards, our wonderful translator and troubleshooter.

Sometimes, in discussing this topic, you hear comments along the lines of music being a 'universal language' – something like: 'When I spoke to them they, like, didn't understand what I was, like, saying, cos they speak Chinese, and I, like, don't. But, like, when I played my viola, they understood exactly what I was trying to say. Y'know what I mean?' Actually, it's a bit more complicated than that.

The other day, I found myself shouting upstairs at my teenage son and told him to 'turn that racket down'. This was then followed by a conversation with my wife about how rubbish music is these days, and how it just sounded like a lot of noise, and nobody would be listening to it in thirty years. I passed a mirror, and saw the image of my father. If music were truly a universal language, then we'd all understand every piece of music; and who can honestly say that? (Apart from Pierre Boulez, and even he is confused by Radiohead's last album.) My point is that a lot of the work we do is creative, allowing youngsters not only to perform but to create their own music. This takes an enormous amount of work, time, and especially patience from the players, so you can imagine the mountain they faced going to China. Managed by Discovery's David Nunn, and led by animateur Paul Rissmann, who has the energy of twenty children's TV presenters, the workshops took place in between rehearsals and concerts, leaving the players with no time off to enjoy their jet lag. These guys worked unbelievably hard.

Before the concerts in Shanghai, there were performances by the Discovery team and the young people in the foyer of the concert hall. People crowded round to hear the pieces the young people had written, guided by Paul and the LSO players. The standard of the final performances was very good indeed, although that's not really the point. We rehearse in the LSO to give a good performance; for these kids, the rehearsals or work-shops were an end in themselves, and it was just nice to show everyone what they had been doing. The smiles all round spoke for themselves.

Later that week a large group of us stayed on an extra day in Beijing to do some masterclasses at the music conservatoire with their EOS orchestra. The music school is far bigger and better equipped than most British colleges. We were teaching in a new ten-storey block with literally hundreds of large, airy rehearsal rooms for lessons – it was a stark contrast to the windowless, soul-sucking room in which I had my flute lessons at college.

We didn't have translators, but at least one of the students was an English speaker. Jenny introduced herself and showed me her gold flute, which cost ten times more than my instru-ment. It turned out she had studied in Paris, and I nervously said, '*Ah oui, très bien.*'

She breathed a sigh of relief. '*Parlez-vous français?*' she asked.

'Er, *oui. Un peu?*' I replied uncertainly.

I didn't catch the next paragraph, as she launched into flaw-less French. *Zut alors* – this wasn't going to be as simple as I had thought. It occurred to me that this might be a good time to see whether I was wrong, and music was a universal language after all. In the group were three young women, all with very expensive flutes, and a few observers. I stepped awkwardly into the room, we exchanged smiles, and I got my flute out – all well so far. Normally, when I do classes, I don't like to demonstrate too much; it isn't always helpful, as it is very rarely a good idea to copy someone. Better to take advice, and then find your own way. In Beijing, though, I had no option. We were working on some well-known orchestral excerpts and they were all playing all the right notes, in the right order. The trouble is, once you get to this point in a performance, you have to start developing aspects such as expression, emotion, depth of feeling: all things which are impossible to explain. Particularly, at least for a monolingual English speaker, in Chinese (or French).

So it went like this: 'When you play Daphnis, you have to sound like you are in love, but don't start off too loudly or aggressively. Just like real life, to be honest.' Blank looks. I did a sort of 'I'm in love' mime by crossing my hands over my heart and looking a bit soft. Right, got that bit. 'But don't start too loudly.' Blank looks.

'Er... *piano*? Yes?' Excellent. The student played again, and it did sound better. We moved further through the solo to a point at which the player really needs to ramp up the tension, perhaps increasing the speed of the vibrato. 'At this point you need to sound more persuasive, more insistent. Try thinking about the tone you make here, maybe more direct and focused than earlier.'

More blank looks.

'Er ... *espressivo*?'

She smiled and played.

'Better. *Molto espressivo!*'

She tried again, and got it perfectly. And so we continued for three hours: me waving my arms around, miming, and sometimes dancing around the room, to the amusement of the flautists. All communication was done in Italian musical terms, with a bit of German thrown in for the Mahler excerpts. They didn't speak English, I didn't speak Chinese, but by the end we were all laughing and smiling and understood each other perfectly, despite the vast cultural difference, through music. It was almost as if we had found a universal language ... oh, hang on ...

When the audience finally let us go home after our last concert in Beijing, and we enjoyed an end-of-tour party, it was time to reflect on the trip. I was overwhelmed by the reaction to the concerts, which had been so different from previous visits to China. Although parts of the urban centres look more and more Western these days, often you need only to turn a corner to be transported back in time to the old China, with street vendors selling foods in the Hutongs that even my adventurous stomach cannot contemplate. There were moments when I felt welcome and at home in a strange place, and others when I felt like a visiting alien, but the times when it felt absolutely right were when we were playing and sharing what we do.

The critic Alex Ross writes on his blog *The Rest is Noise* that classical music blogs 'put a human face on an alien culture'. Given the cultural differences between East and West, I am sure that much of what we play in the LSO could most definitely be described as such, and equally sure that a stage full of Westerners playing alien music is a strange sight for many Chinese concertgoers. My experience this week showed me, however, that music is certainly a language; one that allows people the world over to appreciate and engage with unfamiliar forms very quickly. I am not sure it can ever truly be a universal language in the purest sense, but it's the closest thing we have.

Lost

The familiar feeling of weightlessness, combined with the sense of an out-of-body experience, tells me that we are in Japan once again. No matter how many times I come here, I never get used to the jet lag, which was enhanced this time by our daytime flight (actually two days). I spent the first night sleeping soundly thanks to the effort of getting here, but after our first day in Osaka I felt the familiar combination of tiredness and inability to sleep. I switched my laptop on and tuned into my local radio station back home, which informed me that there were major travel problems in London. Even this gave me little comfort.

On my day off, as it was raining, I went to the fantastic aquarium in Osaka. It really is incredible: you find yourself descending around the biggest tank I have ever seen, with seals, dolphins, and basking sharks. It is a very magical place, with my favourite bit being the room full of tanks of jellyfish bathed in ultra-violet light. In my altered state, the soft music and the strange creatures dancing gracefully underwater were surreal. In the large tank was a diver, doing what I thought was routine cleaning. They are very big on the delicate balance of the ecosystem at this place; there are messages everywhere about saving coral reefs and the plight of the plankton. It is a place that takes itself and its work very seriously. It was with some surprise, therefore, that as the diver got closer I realized that he wasn't doing any cleaning at all – he was waving madly at the people on the other side of the tank, through the glass. I stayed to watch until he came round to my side of the tank. As he approached, the children around me became very excited, and I then realized why: the diver was dressed up as Father Christmas, with red suit, beard, and even a sack covering his oxygen cylinder. I bowed to peer pressure and waved at him, grinning like an idiot. My daughter would have asked where the chimney was. The fish seemed unmoved.

For a country that, in general, doesn't celebrate it, Christmas is everywhere – the sparkly, celebratory aspect of the holiday, rather than the religious point. Just as on any British high street, in fact. Japan and Paris are linked in the strange map of my mind. They have in common the fact that if you change one tiny part of a word or inflect it slightly wrongly you can find yourself endlessly repeating it, ever more slowly and loudly, in an attempt to make yourself understood. In Paris, I think this is a game that they play with tourists from time to time; but the people in Japan are very polite, and despite my own inadequacies in the Japanese language, it is amazing how far you can get with a little *please, thank you,* and bowing. I have been into many shops and left with an aching face simply from smiling.

Today, at a station office, I asked where I had to change to go to Osakako. I pronounced this so that the end of the word rhymed with 'whacko'. The two ladies behind the desk giggled, and conferred: no idea where I was talking about, evidently. I tried again. No luck. I attempted to say that I was going to the aquarium, in the hope that this might help; it didn't. I found myself doing a sort of 'fishy' movement with my hand, and a matching mouth impression. Still no luck. I then pulled from my pocket a Japanese subway map upon which the hotel concierge had circled station C16. I showed the giggling ladies my map, pointed to C16 and said, for the final time before giving up and getting a taxi, 'to Osakako'. They chorused, 'Ahhh: Osakak-*O*.' The *O* sound at the end was slightly longer than I had used, thus rendering my pronunciation totally unintelligible. Or maybe it was my fish impressions that made them want to detain me further. I bowed, thanked them, and left them giggling behind me.

I was recounting this story at the end of the day, and musing on whether we were like this in London when people mispronounced names. Did it make us unable to understand them like this? Surely not? I was put in my place when Bryn told me about his visit to the opticians that day in Japan. He'd had to make a visit to fix his glasses, and managed to find an optician who spoke English. Well, sort of, but an awful lot better than our Japanese. So, what was the problem? I asked. 'Well,' he said, 'It was going fine, and we were talking about places he had visited in Europe, but he spoke very fast in English and it was difficult to understand what he said.'

I asked him if there was anything in particular.

'Well, at the end we couldn't tell whether he had said he was part Italian, his partner was Italian, or he had an Italian passport.'

Crutches, concertos, and Switzerland

This weekend we made a brief stopover in Rotterdam before embarking on the main part of the tour to Switzerland. The schedule this week is such that we hardly ever seem to be staying in the city where we are actually playing; for instance, as I write this, I am sitting on my balcony in Montreux overlooking Lake Geneva, despite the concert taking place tonight in Geneva. It is the kind of view that writers and composers would kill for to inspire great symphonies. Literary giants would summon up paragraphs of descriptive prose that would describe the vista for centuries to come. Quite simply, it's a lovely view.

Touring is a little tricky for me this week, as I had a small accident the other day while out running and tore ligaments in my ankle, which has meant hobbling around with a crutch for a while. Sadly, although this has curtailed my running, it still leaves me able to play the flute.

Unfortunately, Emanuel Abbühl, our principal oboe who was to have played the Mozart concerto last night, was too ill to perform. (He wasn't running with me; it was something else.) When the promoter came on to announce it there was an audible sound of disappointment from the audience, particularly as Emanuel is Swiss. It was then announced that we would instead be playing Mahler 10. There was a mixture of gasps, laughing and applauding. I grant you, it's not the obvious replacement for a Mozart oboe concerto, but it's what we had with us, as we play it at the end of the week. I did wonder, though, whether he had explained that we were playing only the first movement and not the whole hour-long piece. That would have been a very long concert indeed. As luck would have it, today is the 100th anniversary of Mahler's death, and so although we won't be playing Mozart with Emanuel, we will be at least marking a centenary.

Switzerland is a very interesting country: yesterday, in Bern, most people seemed to be speaking German, but here in Montreux French seems to be the predominant language, with a bit of Italian thrown in. On arrival at Zurich airport, I was waiting for my suitcase when the tannoy system crackled into life: '*Meine Damen und Herren ...*'.

I got the gist of it I thought, but my German isn't great. Then it continued: '*Mesdames et messieurs ...*'. Then the same thing in Italian, by which time I was one of only a few people left waiting for a bag. This announcement was taking ages. I have to admit to being a bit nervous; I thought perhaps I had missed a security alert and should have evacuated during the German bit.

Finally: 'Ladies and Gentlemen, welcome to Zurich. Please do not leave your luggage unattended at any time, as this can cause unnecessary delays in transit.'

What a relief: running on crutches is a nightmare.

Paul McCartney isn't HIP any more

Given the title of this section, you might imagine that we are working with one of our slightly more leftfield acts: Grizzly Bear, Nitin Sawhney, Hugh Masakela. You would be mistaken. Note the careful use of capitalization in the title: HIP. Not a financial product, I promise; it stands for Historically Informed Performance.

What we are doing is playing Beethoven, conducted and instructed by Sir John Eliot Gardiner. I should make it clear now that I enjoy working with him, and I enjoy the way he asks us to play. Make no mistake: if you come to hear us, you will hear a very different sound from the recordings we made with Haitink a few years ago (though I would never say that one was superior to another). When we first started working in this way a few years ago, there was a steep learning curve for most of us. I was used to playing in the LSO; I was used to the sound we made when we performed Mahler, Strauss, and Brahms. I even knew how we usually performed Beethoven and Mozart. Then John Eliot turned up and demanded that we play with little or, in my case, no vibrato. This is a lot harder than it sounds. Having worked on playing in a particular way for so many years and tried to make my vibrato an integral part of my sound, much like a singer, I suddenly had to switch it off. Of course, when I did, all the little inadequacies in my playing were exposed. I was astonished to find that previously smooth, long, arched phrases were now lumpy, disjointed fragments of music, which I disliked enormously.

Privately I blamed the style, and looked forward to being able to switch the wobble back on again. But it became apparent that the lumpen phrasing I was now producing was due to previously using said wobble like a musical Pritt Stick; where there were gaps and holes in the tone, I could simply smudge the edges. It was like having a Photoshopped picture of a supermodel suddenly stripped back to its original state. (I am in no way comparing myself to a supermodel. I know my limitations.) It felt like the goalposts had not so much been moved, but ripped up and put on the pitch over the road. 'Whaddaya mean, I can't play Beethoven the way I normally do?'

Gradually, as we worked on different attacks to notes, actually playing what was in the parts rather than received versions, it became clear that music that I had long taken for granted was having the dust blown off. I found myself putting in huge amounts of effort, and the results were truly exciting. For instance, the excitement this week of playing No. 9 with the Monteverdi choir is immense. The choir, John Eliot's own choir, is the choral equivalent of *Doctor Who*'s TARDIS: there are only 36 of them, but when they open their mouths, they make the sound of over 200. The tempi are a little quicker than you might be used to; the sound of the orchestra is not the sound of Gergiev's LSO, but sleeker and more chiselled. It is sometimes just as loud, but in a more punctuated way.

For instance, Nigel Thomas, our timpani player, is playing calf-head timps with very hard sticks. When he explodes in No. 9 or in the storm in No. 6, the sound is of shattering proportions: immediate, concentrated, and thrilling. Hearing the gently throbbing, vibrato-less sound of the strings at the start of the slow movement of No. 6 is a beautiful moment that conjures up the sound of the river burbling away. I really enjoy this way of playing, and the LSO has always had a chameleon-like ability to move between styles – this is no different.

It is worth noting that Nigel is once again playing on the same kind of drum skins that would have been used in 1912, not to mention in Beethoven's time. The calf heads are still just as susceptible to the changes in climate on tour, although the type of drums used are the modern equivalent. A century ago, Charles Turner would laboriously have had to tune using a series of pegs around the circumference of the drum; Nigel, however, is able to use a hydraulic pedal system, which is quicker and allows him to tune the timpani to different notes. Funnily enough, Charles had lunch in Chicago with a Mr Ludwig, who invented the modern system that is now almost universally used. He mentions it in his diary entry of April 21st: 'Meet the Mr Ludwig.

See his patent tuning hydraulic drums. Very fine but too small in depth.'

It would seem that if Turner were alive today, he might be surprised to see this system being used. But using modern timpani with old-fashioned heads: does that qualify as 'Historically Informed Performance'? John Eliot and others like him have uncovered a huge wealth of knowledge and research over the years on the style of performance and the types of techniques used during Beethoven's time. A lot of painstaking work has gone into investigating the types of instruments, the sounds, the way musicians interpreted the markings in a score, and so on. I am not sure that every conductor who specializes in this type of work agrees on all points (just listen to the difference in period performances from 30 years ago and now), but there certainly is a style, which is now taught in various ways at music colleges everywhere.

When John Eliot works with us, he doesn't expect us to throw away our modern instruments and pick up classical violins and flutes, blow the cobwebs off Charles Turner's timpani, wear sandals and eat lentils. He does expect us to incorporate some historical techniques into our performance. I don't have a problem with any of this, although you do have to make a leap of faith with it. The image of a dinosaur in *Jurassic Park* is simply an interpretation – we have only skeletal remains in general, and we don't know exactly how they moved, sounded, or even what colour they all were. Similarly, we don't have recordings from Beethoven's time, and written descriptions of performances differ greatly – it's rare for the same concert to be described by critics in the same way, even today. Interpretation still has a huge part to play. That, for me, is why the performances with John Eliot are so exciting: we read the rule book, we adapt it to our instruments, and we give a new interpretation which will be different to any other. Historically informed.

I was thinking about this the other day when I was driving with the radio on and the Beatles were singing 'Back in the USSR'. Following on from the previous, more recent song, the Beatles sounded (whisper it) a bit tinny and underpowered, their voices rather reedy. I put on a CD I got for Christmas of Sir Paul McCartney playing live in New York, recorded in the last few years. He performs the same song, and on it his voice has grown richer with age; the drum part is more complex, the guitars now form a wall of sound. In short, it is not historically informed at all, but a change from the original that has developed over many years of performance and technological improvements in electric instruments. As it is the original writer playing it, of course, he can do what he wants. No doubt if John Lennon were still alive and playing the same song, it would be something else again. Who knows how it might sound, performed in 100 years' time? Ultimately, it doesn't really matter that much. We don't play Strauss the same way that Strauss originally heard it. Certainly the sound of Elgar conducting Elgar with the LSO doesn't sound like the LSO recording of Elgar with Sir Colin Davis. All these interpretations have gradually evolved, and evolved differently around the world. It doesn't sound better or worse, just different, and each person will undoubtedly prefer one or the other. Diversity in music, historically informed or not, is a wonderful thing; it's just nice to be part of an ensemble capable of leaping from one style to the other with relative ease.

12 Arthur Nikisch
12 October 1855 – 23 January 1922
1912

Arthur Nikisch was one of the greatest conductors of his age. Born in Hungary in 1855, he began his career at the opera in Leipzig, where he became principal conductor before the age of 30. Later, he was principal conductor of the Boston Symphony Orchestra. In 1895 he became principal conductor of both the Berlin Philharmonic and the Leipzig Gewandhaus Orchestras, where he remained until his death.

Nikisch is often described as the first truly modern conductor: he took the study of scores to a new level of complexity and depth. He was known for giving a simple, clear beat and using his eyes to communicate his wishes to players. Conductor George Szell said that 'he was in the best sense hypnotic and magic. You could not extricate yourself from his spell.' Continuing his mystical theme, he also called him an 'orchestral wizard'.* Fritz Reiner, another great conductor of the twentieth century, described the influence he had on his own style, 'It was [Nikisch] who

---

* *The Great Conductors* by Harold C. Schonberg. London: Simon and Schuster, 1967.

told me that I should never wave my arms in conducting, and that I should use my eyes to give cues'.* As well as influencing young conductors, he also impressed composers with his skill and musicality with the orchestra. Tchaikovsky said, 'He doesn't seem to conduct, but rather exercise some mysterious spell.' At a performance of Brahms's Fourth Symphony in Leipzig in 1895, the composer was in the audience, and remarked in a letter to his publisher Fritz Simrock shortly afterwards that Nikisch's interpretation was, 'Quite exemplary, it's impossible to hear it any better.'†

In many ways, Nikisch deliberately cultivated his aura. He was one of the first conductors to recognize the importance of showmanship in a performance. He was meticulous with his appearance: his clothes were always closely fitted to emphasize the graceful contours of his body as he worked, his delicate hand movements framed by elaborate lace cuffs. He was renowned for conducting everything from memory. At the time, audiences were hugely impressed by this seemingly impossible feat, which left him able to use his mesmeric eyes to great effect.

There is a wonderful article, published in the *New York Times* on April 8th 1912 before the LSO tour began, entitled 'Shudders over Schoenberg'. In it, Nikisch again relates how sorry he is that he ever left America, and how happy he is to be back. The interviewer then asks him about the state of contemporary music, and he describes his admiration for Strauss – in particular his new opera, *Der Rosenkavalier.* He also expresses his admiration for the music of Debussy: 'He in his way is a great revolutionist, but he has succeeded in writing beautiful music, even if it is different.'

---

* *Fritz Reiner: A Biography* by Philip Hart. Illinois: Northwestern University Press, 1994.

† *Johannes Brahms: Life and Letters.* Edited by Styra Avins. Oxford: OUP, 1997.

Arthur Nikisch in 1912.

However, when asked whether he values the work of Schoenberg, Nikisch throws his hands in the air. 'If that is music then I do not know music. I cannot think of Schoenberg as anything but a bluff. He is trying to see how far he can go. A child could compose music as good.' The interviewer continues to ask him if he thinks that Schoenberg is the future of music. Nikisch replies, 'If it is and I had to conduct music of that character I should change my occupation.' The music he would be bringing on tour with the LSO was all tried and tested, with no novelties. Although taking the art of conducting to new levels, he wasn't particularly interested in pushing the musical landscape further in certain directions.

In 1912, newspapers around the country were filled with details of 'the $1,000-a-night conductor'. He not only seemed to cast a spell over the orchestra, but over audiences as well. Reviews mention his eyes, his shock of hair, his elegant dress, and his deeply searching and profound musical interpretations. He was frequently stopped on the street by admirers desperate to kiss his hand, and the adulation he received peaked at the final concert in New York. The *New York Times* had this to say on April 30th:

WOMEN CHEER NIKISCH:
Wildly Wave Handkerchiefs at Last Concert of London
Symphony

The scenes at the last New York concert of the London Symphony Society yesterday afternoon [...] were not those ordinarily to be observed at a symphony concert. It was, in fact, distinctly the day of the virtuoso, and Arthur Nikisch was the virtuoso. Storms of applause greeted him after every number which he conducted, and at the end of the concert women rushed down the aisles to the front waving their handkerchiefs and cheering [...] Time after time he was called out to bow his thanks before the audience would leave.

Note that this is no review of the concert – that appeared later in the paper; this was the stuff of the gossip columns.

In keeping with his position as the leading example of a new type of conductor, Nikisch employed a press agent long before the spin doctors of our age became the norm. When he was asked about the significance of the rather large sapphire ring that he wore on his left hand, his agent stepped in and described how, after a concert in Germany, he was given a package in which the ring was wrapped inside a programme from that evening's performance. On the programme was written, in a feminine hand, 'Wear this in memory of an unknown admirer.'

And so, the press agent continued, Nikisch wears it in memory of *all* women. A headline in the *Milwaukee Journal* of April 14th summed him up succinctly:

NIKISCH IS CLIMAX

Quite.

I3 Conducting a Conversation
2012

Bernard says ...

A *Guardian* article in 2009 about conductors, charming in its way, detailed the long history of confrontation between players and *maestri*, and was intent on showing how overinflated the latter's fees are. We could argue about that for ever, but very little of it mirrored my experience.[*]

By the time we reach a concert, a great deal of hard work has been done in rehearsal, and a large part of the conductor's role is to inspire. An odd assertion by the *Guardian* contributor, herself an orchestral musician, is that during a concert she barely has time to look up to see the beat, as she has too much to do. She also suggests that the success of the concert is pretty much down to the players, with very little input from the conductor.

---

[*] http://www.guardian.co.uk/commentisfree/2009/oct/06/orchestral-conductors-pay-cut

Hmm; not with Bernard on the podium. Any discussion over the level of difference a conductor makes could probably be settled by comparing the LSO playing Mahler 9 with Haitink on one night and with Gergiev on another. I'm sure listeners will have their own personal favourite, but I don't think anyone would say that we sound the same!

I thought of this during one of our rehearsals in Avery Fisher Hall recently. Google Bernard Haitink, and you'll find hundreds of articles containing phrases like 'economical gestures' and 'man of few words'. Haitink doesn't always say much, but he shows so much with his conducting; and when he does speak, a few words make a huge difference.

Schubert 5 is one of my favourite symphonies: it gives me a tremendous feeling of happiness, a bit like a child waking up on Christmas morning, as we dance through the first movement. Just as enthusiasm sometimes overtakes good manners when the child unwraps the stocking, it's easy to start ripping the paper off a little too fast. In one rehearsal, you could sense that the orchestra was getting a little too over-excited for the simplicity of line Bernard wanted. He stopped us.

'OK, these accents on the bar-lines are a little too much now, yes? Nothing harsh, just a little bow to Schubert please. Once more.'

And that was it. A small sentence with a huge impact – we all knew what he meant. Other conductors might have to sing what they wanted, or go to great lengths to explain how the accent was to sound. Bernard just wants a nod in the right direction. In this respect he is very like Sir Colin, in that he trusts the players' judgement as well as his own.

The opening of the slow movement is quite tricky, and Bernard was anxious that we do it quickly enough, otherwise 'it sounds boring already'. So we played it and he smiled. He graciously stopped us at the first repeat mark.

'Well, that really was very good indeed ... let's do it again to make sure!'

We repeated it.

'Yes, good, but please, *pi-an-iss-i-mo*. Don't get louder, yes?'

We repeated it again, this time with Bernard barely moving.

'Yes. As I thought. The less I do, the better it sounds.'

We all laughed. 'It's because you must listen more.'

And there you have it. You can have one of the greatest conductors in the world in front of you, but if you don't listen, it means nothing.

There are times when Gordan Nikolitch, our leader, speaks to the orchestra. If Bernard comes from the Harold Pinter school of dialogue, then Gordan takes Eric Cantona as his role model. Last week in rehearsal, we stopped and Gordan said, 'Sorry, Bernard, may I say something?'

Bernard settled back on his stool and watched intently as Gordan spoke. I sometimes find it hard to hear exactly what he says, as he is a long way away, and he often talks and plays at the same time, demonstrating the kind of sound he is after.

'Hey, guys, listen to the sound here. It's kind of (*demonstrates the sound*) *waaaaah*, you know what I mean? But you know, we need like (*demonstrates a different sound*) *waaaeeeerrr*, you know what I mean? I mean, less hard, more like Swiss cheese, you know what I mean?'

I assume the first violins knew what he meant. Gordan turned around and nodded at Bernard to show that he was finished and he could resume the rehearsal.

Bernard raised his eyebrows and started again. The sound was indeed different. We stopped again.

'Well, Gordan, I didn't understand a word of what you said, but they do. That is exactly the sound I am after.' He turned to the leader of the second violins, David Alberman.

'He did say Swiss cheese, didn't he?'

'Er, yes, Maestro, he did.'

'OK.'

During the opening concert last night, I made a point of noting how often I looked up. I wanted to see if I really was too busy to watch. The truth is, I spent most of the time watching Bernard's every gesture as he moulded and crafted the performance. A lot of the time, Bernard seems to be enjoying the sound of the band: a look of approval when the remarkable Phil Cobb sails above the texture, or a smile at the characteristic playing of Lorenzo; and there is a huge amount of affection for him from us, too. I can't wait for the next two shows.

I'm sure, as in all things, there are overpaid conductors. But there is no question about it in my mind: Bernard is priceless.

Oh, Vienna ...

The famous 1980s hit 'Vienna' by Ultravox (possibly the greatest song never to reach number one in the UK charts) has always puzzled me – perhaps simply because I can never remember any of the lyrics other than that one classic line.

There is an atmosphere in Vienna, the most famous of musical centres: the ghosts of Mozart, Mahler, and Strauss, perhaps, or the turbulent history of the area? Whatever it is, Vienna feels like nowhere else in Europe. Music and all its paraphernalia are everywhere, from the street names to the food (Mozart Risotto, anyone?), right down to the men in period cloaks inviting you to endless candlelit performances of Mozart classics in 18th-century churches. You can visit one of Mozart's houses, which has been stripped back to its earlier plasterwork and fitted out with glass cabinets of artefacts and facsimiles, and looks a little like one of those demonstration rooms you find at Ikea. The smell of horses is never far away, as the city is full of open carriages and all that goes with that mode of transport. This probably accounts for the luxuriant displays of flowers in the summer months. However, we are not here as tourists; we are here to work, and this time Valery is at the controls.

Our home at the Barbican is not the most reverberant of concert halls, and consequently we have to work hard to make a good sound. Playing at the Musikverein, with its famously luxuriant acoustic, we can sound overwhelming. Strauss's *Ein Heldenleben* is a detailed and complex score that demands clarity if it is not to turn to soup, so when we play in Vienna rather than at home, in the Barbican, it requires a different approach. As Richard Strauss himself used to conduct this piece in this very hall, there is no excuse not to get it right – in fact, it is vitally important that we do.

Valery spends much of the balance rehearsal doing what it says: balancing the score. The Musikverein has such a character of its own that it almost becomes another instrument in the orchestra. The long chord at the end of the piece, in which the wind and brass have to diminuendo, is made much easier; however, the rich opening with its multiple lines and rhythms can be a messy sludge. By the time the concert arrives, Valery is a more contained version of himself in terms of movement, and urges restraint in dynamics from the heavy artillery of the orchestra. Once we do this the sound is fabulous: there is one moment in particular near the end of the piece where the strings soar up to a high phrase – it is simply one of the most beautiful sounds I have ever heard, and I can't help but smile. Stravinsky's *Petrushka* is also on the programme. I love playing this with Valery. I don't know any other conductor who can conjure up images from the ballet like he does. In rehearsal we reached the flute cadenza, which is where the ballerina begins to dance; I played it as I thought it should go. Valery stopped.

'Gareth, that level of virtuosity is not needed here; he is a street magician who picks up a flute. Take your time.'

Sure enough, the bit immediately preceding the cadenza took on a different form as he conducted it and suddenly the cadenza (something that I've never been quite sure how to play) made sense. There's a famous episode in which a bear (played by the tuba) comes to market, and the clarinets screech away to call the crowds in. It's a difficult bit to play, as the two clarinets have to play very high in unison, but today it sounded very good indeed. Valery stopped.

'*Clarinetti.* It sounds too good. I want more like a glissando instead of hearing all the notes. Don't forget, he is holding his clarinet in one hand playing, and in the other hand he is holding a chain with a bear on it. I don't know about you, but I wouldn't be concentrating on playing it evenly!'

Fair point. It is the attention to detail that he brings to this ballet music that makes it such a joy to play with him and this is why, following the ballet's downbeat ending at the close of the concert, the audience in Vienna was stunned into silence before applauding at length.

Leaving the stage, I saw posters for the performances of great artists, past and present, at the Musikverein. I passed a bust of Gustav Mahler, and felt the weight of musical history mixed with a sense of relief at the success of the performance.

It means nothing to me?

It means everything.

The one where I ate a lot and played a little Mozart

I read in the *New York Times*, while eating a large American breakfast, that in twenty years' time, over 65% of the Western world will be clinically obese. Never being one to waste time, I have reached this stage in the space of about three hours, and six courses. We've just got back from Maze, Gordon Ramsay's new restaurant here in New York. Despite the name, we found our table very easily and decided on the chef's menu of six courses.

Six small courses sounded like the perfect amount – not too much, not too little – and I was doing fine until the last spoonful of my dessert (peanut butter sandwich with a strawberry sorbet – an Elvis homage, presumably) when I suddenly realized I was stuffed to the gills. It reminded me of going to see Wagner's *Ring*: you sit and wallow in the high-cholesterol, well-upholstered beauty of the music. You sit, in fact, for a very long time. Then, just when you think it's all over, the fat lady sings. This is when you realize that clichés aren't always true, as there are in fact another seven hours of opera to follow. It's only when you get home, slightly stiff and unsure whether you really enjoyed it or not, that you realize how much money it's cost you.

Bryn Lewis (harp) and Joost Bosdijk (bassoon) trying to order.

I think I'll have some fruit for lunch tomorrow.

At three o'clock, after a quick dash around the shops, we convened at the hall with Sir Colin and Imogen Cooper to rehearse the Mozart concerto for tomorrow night. The piece really does have a chamber music kind of feel, particularly between the piano and woodwind. The soloist was anxious to see me, as we have quite a few bits to play together, but being vertically challenged, I was lost behind cellist Tim Hugh's head and she couldn't make eye contact. 'I need to be able to see your eyes in the first movement,' she explained. (Blimey, it's a while since anyone's said that.)

Sir Colin was on his usual marvellous form: he is undeniably in charge, but has a way of making us feel we can play however we wish. Whenever I play with Sir Colin, he encourages and inspires. If you have a solo, he never dictates how you should play it but, somehow, he gets you to play it just how he wants it. Magic, I suppose. However, he never wants to take credit for anything. You will have noticed, if you have seen him at the end of a concert, that he never wants to take a solo bow: he always wants applause for the band. Equally, he very rarely singles out individual players for bows. It's as if he is captain of a team, and we all work together.

Birthday parties, Christmas parties, and another concert

Looking at my schedule while drinking a coffee on Broadway, I was reminded of a kid I went to school with whose birthday was Christmas Day.

No doubt you remember that, when you are seven, your birthday has huge significance, as does Christmas. It was all about the presents when I was tiny. On your birthday, you'd get some presents and maybe a party, and if you were really lucky, more presents from the guests at the party. At Christmas, we had presents from Mum and Dad and Father Christmas – in short, lots of presents. My birthday is in October. This boy at school, because he had his birthday on Christmas Day, always got one big present for both Christmas and birthday. When you are six or seven, it's about quantity rather than quality, so we always felt a little sorry for him. He never had a birthday party, either; or maybe I just wasn't invited.

A recent review of a concert in the *New York Times* discussed the relationship between Sir Colin and us, the players. I have been very lucky to be in the orchestra during what critics repeatedly call his 'Indian summer'. I don't like this description at all: it seems to indicate some sort of quiet, mellow, smiling old man at the helm, and Colin is nothing of the sort. Where I sit, I can see his eyes twinkle with mischief and rage in Beethoven, propel Berlioz along with an unstoppable energy, and give Sibelius an urgency like no other. It's not an Indian summer – it's more like being on a roller coaster driving through a forest fire. And now Valery is our new principal conductor, so different from Colin in every way, except for the passion for music that they share. I love working with him, too, and again I can't quite believe that I am in the orchestra with him on the box. It's incredible.

Looking through our schedule for the next year, I see that we have fantastic work with Valery, continuing with his Mahler cycle, as well as some more wonderful work with Colin. It seems almost greedy to have so much time with two of the greatest conductors of our age – a bit like we've got Christmas and our birthday all at once. Except, unlike the kid at school, we get to have two big presents. And, boy, are we having a hell of a party!

During rehearsal this morning we briefly went through some

bits of the *Eroica* and then rehearsed the Fourth Piano Concerto with pianist Paul Lewis. This was a piece we recorded two weeks ago with Evgeny Kissin, and I am astonished at how different a piece can sound with two different soloists. I studied at the Guildhall School of Music and Drama at the same time as Paul, who, like most pianists, spent much of his time locked away in a practice room. I can confirm, however, that this did pay off: he is much better at the piano than me. Actually, he is marvellous: he brings such freshness and clarity to the piece. I'm really looking forward to the concert tonight. I'm not in the second movement, and it gives me a chance to sit back and not count bars; to rest and enjoy the music.

Coming home for Christmas

At last we have come to the end of a long tour, and it's time to go home. We left Tokyo after nine days of rehearsals, concerts, sightseeing, and shopping. Several people seem to have purchased new, bigger suitcases simply to fit in all of the gifts. Fortunately my origami Christmas decorations (not a joke) don't take up much room, so I am coming home with the same bag.

We have a vast collection of luggage labels, as well. There is the yellow LSO label, a Kajimoto management label, a bag number label, my own label with my name and phone number on it, a label from all of the hotels we stayed in (about six, I think) and various bar-code thingies from flights. My case doesn't know whether it's coming or going. First violinist Maxine Kwok-Adams has a 'heavy' label on her case, the badge of a serious shopper. We also get the labels from airports, the ones with the stickiest glue known to man, which they wrap round your handle: I like spotting them in airports, as they tell you where people are going. They usually have the name of the airport as three letters:

Second violins in Japan.

Heathrow is LHR, Gatwick LGW. My favourite is when we go to Madrid, and the whole band is walking round with luggage labels which say MAD. (You don't have to be, but ... you know the rest.)

Yesterday we flew to Fukuoka, which is in the south and was warm enough to walk around in a T-shirt in December. It is famous for its ramen noodles, which I can tell you are lovely. It was pleasant wandering around the river in the sunshine before the rehearsal, but I was packed and anxious to get on so that I can come home. Time can pass very slowly at the end of a tour; I have yet again missed both my boys' birthdays, and I know it's a lot colder in England now.

The concert was a good one. Valery was in one of his 'let's try something different' moods – and we all watched him like hawks, because you simply cannot rely on the music being the same as the night before. Very exciting. I wasn't in the second half of the show, but when I heard the encore being played, I made my way backstage to get my flute and suitcase ready to get a seat on the bus. As the orchestra was playing the march, I looked over and saw Valery standing offstage, smiling from ear to ear. He had, it appeared, started the orchestra and walked off, leaving them to play on their own, much to the amusement of the audience. I went over to him and said, 'There's a guy who looks just like you conducting in there.'

'Oh, no, there isn't!' he replied, and we both stood looking through the window onto the stage at the orchestra, smiling.

Super-conductor D(SC)H

After winter in the Far East, we were delighted to arrive in Daytona Beach for some time in the sun and some great concerts. The second half of the concert this evening was devoted to Brahms's First Symphony. It's one of my favourite pieces, and a joy to play. Daniel Harding is the conductor in residence this year, and he seems to be enjoying himself. In fact, in the programme for the festival he is described as the 'European

Gareth Davies plays, with Daniel Harding conducting.

super-conductor'. I always thought that was something to do with quantum mechanics, but Dan doesn't seem to mind: he's so relaxed, he's probably following the path of least resistance anyway. Whatever you call him, he does make the symphony very exciting. The audience gave us a standing ovation, which was our cue to move next door for a party, where we all danced to a fabulous big band.

This morning, I managed to sit by the pool for a while before our rehearsal; however, it was soon time to head to the huge arena opposite the hotel for the LSO Pops concert. Tonight's theme was speed: *Flight of the Bumble Bee* was the second piece, followed by a bit from *Harry Potter* where the woodwind players zoomed around like flying broomsticks, musically speaking. But the prize for the night has to go to Carmine Lauri, our leader. He stood up in front of a sea of people and played Paganini's *Moto Perpetuo* unbelievably fast – his fingers were a blur. I saw him afterwards by the pool, drinking a beer: well deserved, but I did wonder if he was dipping his fingers in the water to cool them down when nobody was looking.

I am writing this in bed, despite some of my friends going out. Tomorrow it's my turn up the front: harpist Bryn Lewis and I are the soloists in the first half, playing Mozart's Flute and Harp Concerto, or as it's known here, the *Flat and Sharp*. I don't get to stand up at the front very often, so I am nervous – no, terrified, actually; and, to make matters worse, we have Mahler 1 in the second half. Before that, however, I have one of my regular pre-concert talks to give. Normally on these occasions, I talk about the music that we are performing and conduct an interview with the soloist ... as even I can't talk to myself for 45 minutes, I'll be having a chat about harps and strings and things with Bryn before the show.

Flat and sharp

I woke up with that familiar nauseous feeling in the pit of my stomach. After a few seconds, I remembered why and crawled out of bed, opened the curtains and let the low, blazing sun light up my room. The music for the concerto sat staring at me on the table and the cadenzas, which suddenly seemed to have more notes than before, spilled out of the score.

My flute sat expectantly, waiting to be polished and cleaned, and a clean white shirt hung, crumpled, on a hanger. I ironed it and got ready as fast as I could, wanting to eat some breakfast before nerves prevented me from eating lunch. No time to sit by the pool: we had a morning rehearsal, and then I would be playing the Mozart Flute and Harp Concerto with Bryn Lewis. At that moment, however, I felt more like walking out into the waves and waiting for the sharks.

I managed to eat something, and walked over to the Peabody early to warm up. It's funny how the anticipation of something like this is often worse than the event itself: as soon as I put my instrument together and began playing, I felt calmer. Maybe it was the sense of relief that I could actually play, or maybe it was just doing something, anything, to occupy my mind. In the heat of the dressing room, a small lizard darted across the chair – did this mean good luck? I don't know, but I've never seen one in the Barbican, that's for sure.

The stage filled, and soon we were rehearsing Mahler for the second half of the afternoon concert. As ever, we had to sort out where to place the offstage trumpets. The first time through, they were too loud, so Daniel asked them to move further away. This sounded better, and Dan asked them to come onto the stage (they have a TV monitor so that they can see the conductor). They appeared at one of the side doors.

'That sounds great – how far away are you?'

Rod Franks replied, 'We moved back to the corridor. We tried to play it from Froggy's Bar across the road, but the cables wouldn't stretch.' Daniel laughed, and called for a break in rehearsal.

I fortified myself with a cup of tea, then another one, and returned to the stage. Bryn was already centre stage with his harp, and I took my place next to him. It's a strange feeling, standing up at the front, and daunting: I know that no critics at any newspaper can compete with my colleagues. But the rehearsal went very smoothly, and we actually finished early. I was feeling strangely calm by this point, and ate a sandwich.

Before we played, Bryn and I had to do our pre-concert talk. I've done quite a few of these over the years, but I think Bryn was more nervous about it than about the concerto; however, once we took the stage, he was a natural. The audience here in Daytona Beach always has lots of questions and today was no exception. We found out that he didn't start playing until he was 18, and owns at least seven harps! By the time the talk was over, we had both relaxed, and the countdown began.

I don't have a ritual before I play, but today there was only time to change and warm up again. The orchestra took the stage, the hall was full, and Bryn and I stood in the wings in darkness with Daniel and Carmine. The door opened and light burst out towards us; Carmine walked into it to applause and the door closed, leaving us in the dark again. Alan Goode, our stage manager, asked if we were ready, but it was a rhetorical question; the door was opened once more, and Bryn and I stepped onto the stage. I imagine this is how rugby players feel when they walk out of the tunnel in Cardiff, except it's quieter.

I could see the front few rows of the audience, but the rest were cloaked in darkness, silent, waiting for us to begin. Three minutes earlier I'd been a bundle of nerves and if someone had told me the concert was cancelled, I wouldn't have minded, but now, with my flute up and ready, I felt relaxed and excited all at the same time. I guess I must be a natural show-off.

It's not really for me to say how it went, but I was quite happy. Bryn was, as ever, marvellous, and having the LSO as a backing band is always going to be a treat. Daniel was, of course, a super conductor, and always game for a laugh. The similarity in looks between him and Bryn had been pointed out earlier on in the week – they wear similar glasses and are about the same height, with roughly the same colour of hair. As we waited for the applause to continue in the wings, Daniel kept on saying, 'Quick, let's swap around.' And so they did. Bryn grabbed Daniel's baton and marched to the podium, where he gave the most extravagant bow I have ever seen, and Daniel and I stood next to the harp with our arms around each other, bowing and giggling like naughty schoolboys. Most of the orchestra were crying at this point, which I can assure you had nothing to do with the slow movement. I think only the front row of the audience noticed ...

This is rabbit ...

Yesterday we were joined by the ladies of the London Symphony Chorus and the young men of Eltham College, for Mahler 3. As is always the case when the orchestra is augmented, a fair amount of the rehearsal is spent moving people around so that they can see and sing properly. We made sure that we rehearsed the choir bits first so that they could have a decent break, as they had travelled on the same day – the kids in particular needed some food.

The soloist Anna Larsson, as she doesn't appear until the last half of the symphony, sings from within the orchestra rather than at the front. This presents problems in several different ways. Normally, when a conductor or soloist comes on stage, there is a clear pathway for them to the left of the first violins. But after the conductor comes on, the strings move back in line and the path disappears, so as Anna came on after the long first movement, there was no pathway. More complicated was the fact that she stood in front of the woodwind, so during the concert, when she made her entrance, she had to tiptoe through the basses and celli to find her chair. During the rehearsal, she sat down right in front of David Pyatt, which wasn't a problem until she stood up to sing, at which point neither of them could see anything at all. So it was decided that she would move further down the line, and she ended up in front of me.

'Don't worry,' said Valery. 'He is very nice man.'

Anna smiled doubtfully, and stood in front of me. All I could see was the big blue bow on the back of her dress. But it was only for two movements, so I followed Sharon instead of Valery. Depending on your point of view, this can be dangerous.

Valery is great with children when they come in to work with us. Many conductors seem to take particular delight in crushing the enthusiasm of youth with criticism, but Valery makes them feel comfortable. You could see the delight on their faces as the whole room applauded them after their number. There were only 32 of them, but they didn't half make a lot of noise. You often can't hear the children's choir in Mahler 3, as they get drowned out by the noise of the women and the orchestra, but not this choir. I turned around to watch them and noticed that to amplify their voices they were all singing with their hands cupped around their mouths, as if they were making an important announcement. Valery finished the movement and smiled at their music director and then smiled at the boys, obviously pleased. 'Yes, boys, well done, very good!'

They all beamed back.

'But be careful with hands.'

He put his hands around his mouth to make a funnel, 'It's like this. Not like this.' He then cupped his hands behind his ears. The boys laughed.

'This ... this is rabbit.'

Look into my eyes ...

I have been sleeping quite well here in Japan but, this morning, I awoke at 4 a.m. I watched CNN cycle the same film a few times and then, at 6 a.m., went for a run around the park. It was minus two degrees, so I was astonished to see about thirty locals and their dogs doing tai chi. (Actually, the dogs mainly watched.) When I go running at home in the Surrey hills, I always avoid dogs; their owners tend to shout 'Don't worry, he's just playing, he wouldn't hurt a fly!' just as the dog nips at my ankles. On this occasion, the dogs were mainly asleep, trying to keep warm, and I was more concerned about a flock of territorial ravens who appeared to live in the park. They dive-bombed me every time I ran past. Some of them were bigger than the dogs.

After this bracing exercise, we clambered aboard a bus. Here is the schedule:

8.00   Leave on buses to airport

9.30   Arrive airport; buy packed lunch

10.30   Depart Sapporo on aeroplane

12.45   Arrive Osaka

13.46   Leave Osaka on train; eat packed lunch

15.02   Arrive Kyoto; walk to hotel

16.15   Leave hotel; catch tube to hall

17.30   Rehearsal

19.00   Concert

I thought about hiring a car and going on a boat cruise just to complete the journey. Michael Palin would be proud. Kyoto, I'm told, is an incredibly beautiful place, but as you can see, we had no time to find this out for ourselves.

And so to the concert. It was the same programme as last night; I was in Prokofiev's *Romeo and Juliet*. Tonight was one of those nights that I love being in this orchestra. As soon as Valery walked onto the stage, I could see the look in his eye, and I knew it was going to be fun.

I don't think I have ever played *Romeo and Juliet* in exactly the same way twice with Valery. I don't know any conductor who shapes the music and the sound of the LSO more than he does: he puts slightly longer pauses in to increase the tension, he takes some languorous tunes more slowly, and some nights he pushes the strings like a Roman charioteer whipping his horses, until I think they can't get any faster. Then they do. The sound he gets from them at the end brings a lump to my throat every time, and to be honest, the nice romantic tunes I get to play are easy to tug at the heartstrings with when my wife is thousands of miles away. Sitting as I do in the middle of the stage, Valery is right in front of me, and whenever I have an exposed solo or melody to play, he always does something to encourage me to do it in a particular way. I find this so exciting, and I think it shows in the electric way the band plays with him at the front. When he pauses slightly or slows down unexpectedly in a solo, and you follow him, he always grins at you and has a glint in his eye. There really is a sense of making music together as a team. He asks, and we deliver: simple as that. The Kyoto audience roared their approval and

Gergiev and the LSO in concert in Japan.

we played the March from *The Love for Three Oranges*. Crazy Russian humour.

If I had a pound for every time somebody asked me how we follow Valery's famously fluttering hands, I would be a millionaire. The answer is simple: you may all be watching his hands. We, however, are watching his eyes.

There's snow business ...

It's snowing once again. The roads are gritted and clear, and life continues as normal in Munich. The pavements are covered in so much salt, I can feel my blood pressure rising just by walking on them. There is so much grit that the snow looks like ice cream full of chocolate chunks, with an unnervingly grippy surface.

Walking back from the restaurant, Chi and I tried to skid along the main *Platz* like naughty schoolboys, but were unsuccessful. These clever Germans have managed to take all the fun out of the snow. I think they may have used all of our grit supplies as well: in Rathausplatz, there is more of the stuff in a small area than Boris Johnson managed to find for the whole of Greater London. Where I live, on a hill in Surrey, the council never got round to salting our roads, so to get to work we had to borrow some Maldon from the neighbours. But it does look very pretty here: the beautiful buildings in the centre of town look like the icing-sugar-dusted cakes in the bakery, and the warm and inviting cellars with their vaulted ceilings, roaring fires, and local food and beer look especially tempting today. On this whistle-stop tour of Germany, there is never enough time – but maybe after the concert ...

Although the hall in Munich is quite reverberant, it isn't always easy to hear what everyone else is doing on the stage – a bit of a problem. There are plastic discs hanging above our heads, which I think can change the acoustic a bit, although to be honest, I can't hear any difference. John Eliot Gardiner really uses these seating calls to try out different seating arrangements. Last night he moved the horns closer to my section, and in Beethoven 4, Dave Pyatt sat right next to me. I enjoy this aspect of working with John Eliot. He'll often start the rehearsal with the overture, and then jump down off the stage to walk around the hall, listening. Then he'll jump back up and ask the leader to jump down and listen. When he is happy with the arrangement, we will often just play through a few bits that didn't go as well as we would have liked, and then go off to get changed.

On this occasion I trotted off down the road to the nearest Irish pub with Alan, our Irish stage manager, to watch Wales (hopefully) beat the English. Being half Welsh and half English, I can't really lose but, in all honesty, my shirt is always red. We end up watching a lot of rugby matches from abroad; I remember a very memorable match we watched at 2 a.m. in Beijing a few years ago. Alan and I had already planned to watch the final match of the Six Nations at midnight in a bar in Chicago – but this time we were both singing from the same hymn sheet. Frustratingly, I had to leave ten minutes into the second half, when the outcome was far from decided, to be on stage for the overture. I was promised the final score by text message as soon as it happened.

The hall was full, and I spotted Anne-Sophie Mutter in the audience as well as Madge from *Neighbours* (although perhaps it could have been her doppelgänger). But it was definitely Anne-Sophie – better play well, I thought. We took to the stage and launched into the overture, and then Beethoven 4. This is one of my favourites, although it has a terrifying opening, in which the woodwind and horns have to hold a unison B flat very quietly for what seems like hours. All went very well, and the audience really enjoyed the energy produced in the performance. I really enjoyed the text message that confirmed the Welsh victory.

The second half of the show was our last performance of No. 5, and the orchestra really went for it. Next stop: Leipzig.

We arrived by train. The city still shows a lot of its East German past, and our hotel looked as if it was in the middle of a building site, but the welcome was very warm. Just as well, as it was snowing again. The Gewandhaus is a modern concert hall with a long tradition. The original hall was built in 1781, but the present-day building has been open since 1981. Despite its futuristic appearance, the unbroken historical line of musical tradition is paramount. In case visitors are unaware, the corridors backstage are lined with photographs that stretch back to the early days of the twentieth century. Looking at the pictures of the Gewandhaus orchestra from one hundred years ago in my dressing room, it seems that the LSO of 1912 weren't the only musicians sporting luxurious moustaches. On the approach to the stage there stretches a long line of pictures of their previous principal conductors; at the end of the row, the now familiar face of Arthur Nikisch fixes me with his hypnotic stare.

It is quite an intimidating hall, as the audience is seated all around the orchestra: it felt a little like we were about to be fed to the lions. Some light relief came when Alan Goode and Dan Gobey, our stage managers, had a little trouble with the conductor's rostrum, leading to a brief Laurel & Hardy homage as they both struggled to remove the safety bar from John Eliot's podium – he's such a risk-taker – before eventually giving up; Alan slammed it back down onto the stage. The audience laughed, and applauded them both.

There was a slightly tense atmosphere before we started the piano concerto, as earlier in the rehearsal we had discovered that the piano had been tuned to A=444: far higher in pitch than we play. Much hand-wringing ensued, and finally the tuner was made to bring it down to pitch. It was not until the end of the long first *tutti*, when the piano came in, that we discovered whether he had done it. I felt like Han Solo waiting to see if Obi-Wan had managed to disable the tractor beam in *Star Wars*.

He had.

Dear Father Christmas ...

I have been a good boy this year. I know you are rather busy with all the little kids, but if you get a moment, there are a few things I would really like for myself and my 95 friends.

This year, we have had a bit of a nightmare travelling around the world. Don't worry, I'm not asking for your sleigh or anything – but if you could do some magic, that would help. You remember that volcano earlier this year, when all the airports closed? That was a right pain when we tried to fly. The snow earlier this year even stopped the Eurostar, despite the fact that it goes under the sea. We find it really difficult.

Take, for example, this weekend. We were due to fly to Zagreb on Saturday morning and then Palermo on Sunday morning, and fly back after the concert. I left my house at 5 a.m. and it was minus ten degrees; I slid around the M25 and up the M11 to Stansted. There was already a covering of snow, just enough to look Christmassy. I knew that if we were at all delayed I would be in England long enough to see the newspapers resurrect their snow pun headlines and also to see Sue Mallet, director of planning, spontaneously combust (This would be a bad thing, of course.)

Sir John Eliot Gardiner, who was conducting, was worried about his cows in Dorset. I was worried that if we did get away, we wouldn't get back. We had two sets of instruments going to the two venues, one by air and one by truck, and the charter plane was filled with cellos and violins. It was complicated, even by your standards.

I don't know whether you had anything to do with it, but we took off on time, and it wasn't until we reached Zagreb that we heard about the huge snowfall that had paralysed Britain. Radio and television shouted about TRAVEL CHAOS, and newspaper editors 'dug out' their best puns (see? It's contagious).

The strange thing was that when we landed in Croatia there was loads of snow, and it was much colder than at home, but everybody seemed to be carrying on as normal. The concert was good, and I particularly enjoyed the way John Eliot made the string players stand up to play Mendelssohn's Italian Symphony (apparently that's what they did when it was first played. The basses sort of half stand and half sit anyway on their bar stools, and the cellos didn't stand up, of course; that would have looked silly!) Anyway, if you could sort out the climate for us, that would be grand.

The other thing I would like you to sort out, if you get a chance, is the international instrument transport problem – or, as we call it, the Dijon Syndrome. You may have heard that a few years ago the LSO instruments got stuck on a motorway during a strike, and we all had to borrow instruments from friendly locals and play the concert in Dijon in our jeans. It was something that we didn't want to repeat, and so this weekend we had two sets of instruments – what could go wrong?

As you are pretty much welcome the world over and don't have to worry about visas, carnets, or petrol (although I guess you don't get to collect as many air miles as me), I had better explain a few things. When we travel in the EU, we chuck the instruments in a van and then Dan and Alan drive them to where we are going whilst we stretch out, relax, and live the dream on an economy-class flight. When we get to the hall, we find the van waiting for us, like a homing pigeon. But when we travel outside the EU, we have a thing called a carnet: as I understand it this is a list of all the instruments, probably similar to the billions of letters you get from kids. Miriam, Sue, and Alan take it very seriously indeed. It's like a passport for our instruments, and works well as long as we make sure that we have *only* what is on the list, on the way in and on the way out. It stops us using the LSO as a front for international snare-drum smuggling, which as you can imagine is a huge racket.

This weekend was complicated, as Croatia is not in the EU, but Italy is. As it was such a tight turnaround, we had instruments on one van going to Croatia with a carnet, and another set going to Italy on another van, as well as many people carrying their instruments on the plane. This should have been simple – but it snowed. In northern Italy. As bad luck would have it, Italy turned out to be the *other* country in Europe that cannot deal with snow. What are the chances of that happening?

Unlike you, our van drivers can drive for only a certain number of hours before they have to rest, and despite the fact that they didn't move for six hours this still counted as driving, so we found out in Zagreb that the instruments wouldn't make it to Palermo in time. Dijon Syndrome. But wait a minute, I thought: couldn't we just take the instruments from Zagreb to Palermo, instead? Miriam and Sue looked at me like I was an idiot, and said 'Carnet' in unison. So, despite the fact we had all the instruments we needed for our concert the next day, they had to go back, because they were on the list, and they weren't coming in. To take them off the carnet at this stage would have been illegal, and would have caused Sue Mallet to explode. (Again: this would be a bad thing.) If we took into account the instruments we were

Director of Planning Sue Mallet on her preferred method of transport.

hand-carrying, to perform we still needed to find two violins, two cellos, two trumpets, seven double basses, three trombones, and two timpani (calf-headed, please). On a Sunday in Italy.

I am happy to tell you that a car was dispatched to get some of the smaller items from the van, and we borrowed some timps and basses from the Palermo Opera. We didn't ask you, as you would have been too late.

I hope this list isn't too long, but it is Christmas; and there is one more important thing I would like. If you could keep an eye on my colleagues, please: they all work so hard, and need a bit of looking after, even – and I can't believe I'm going to say this – even the conductors. There were extraordinary scenes this weekend when we played at the opera in Palermo. As I mentioned earlier, the strings were standing for the Italian Symphony, and I'm happy to report that this didn't stop Maxine Kwok-Adams wearing heels so high she was even taller than our leader Roman Simovic, who is 8'6" in his socks. As they were standing, we in the woodwind and brass had extra-high risers, and in Palermo we were about six feet up in the air. I quite liked this but, for a piccolo player, Sharon didn't really enjoy the dizzy heights as much as I thought she would.

Backstage at the opera was a huge area full of props and sets: one side of the room was covered in a massive rock face, and the other side looked as if it was from an opera with a ballroom scene. As we passed through a very small passage to get onto the stage, I couldn't help notice that there was a stage revolver which had just been left on a shelf, presumably for someone to pick up in a fit of rage at the end of (*insert opera of your choice*). The inevitable jokes were made about taking it on stage, or saying it was a shame that (*insert conductor of your choice*) wasn't conducting.

After the interval, the glamorous Palermo audience waited in the glorious surroundings of the opera house for John Eliot. Imagine my surprise when he came striding confidently across the stage brandishing the aforementioned revolver, and pointing it at the audience, too! He then waved it around and pretended to shoot in the air, thereby starting the Italian Symphony at a great lick, like a sprinter from the blocks. Anywhere else, and this kind of thing would possibly have been amusing and slightly surreal; however, although I don't like to deal in stereotypes, it strikes me that the last place you ought to start waving a gun around at the audience is probably Sicily. I quite like John Eliot, and I don't really want to see him sleeping with the fishes just yet. More to the point, I was standing right behind him. I don't mind telling you that Sharon and I ducked – the show must go on, you know. I looked to the wings and saw Sue Mallet looking on in disbelief; she looked as if she was going to explode again (this would be a bad thing).

Funnily enough, it was a tremendously exciting performance, and we dashed back to the airport afterwards to find out whether the TRAVEL CHAOS in Britain was going to allow us to return. I'm happy to tell you that we all got back on time to Stansted Airport, where they had had the brilliant idea of moving the snow off the runway, thereby enabling the planes to take off *and* land. Brilliant. After I had cleared the snow off my car, I trundled around the M25 and finally got to bed at 2.30 a.m., finishing the two-day tour, which felt like a week. It was only when I switched on the news the next day and saw those poor people who had been sleeping for two days at Heathrow that I realized how lucky we had been to go anywhere at all.

One last thing, Father Christmas: I'd like to wish all the staff at LSO Towers a very merry Christmas, and a nice relaxing time away from emails and phone calls.

Best wishes,

Gareth, aged 40-ish

14 A Plague of Locusts
1912

Leaving Boston with their tails between their legs, the LSO found themselves on a train for the rest of the tour, stopping off at various cities for concerts – often two a day, in different towns. Pew's great money-saving idea was sold to the orchestra in a positive light. The train was described as an exclusive Pullman, classed as a 'special', and 'having in view the comfort of the musicians so that they may appear at every concert in the best possible condition'. In reality, this meant that down the sides of each carriage were bunk beds, and in the centre of the train was a buffet car, where most of the orchestra seemed to spend a great deal of time. Charles Turner was quite impressed: 'My first experience in an American Train. Quite all right. Long corridor carriages. The railway stations are very beautiful buildings, like the inside of cathedrals. Great stone halls.'

The end coach was reserved for VIPs such as Nikisch and Pew as well as sponsors of the tour, who would sometimes travel with the orchestra for parts of the journey. Travel was often overnight,

LSO players standing in front of their train at St Louis, 1912.

particularly on days with two concerts; this led to many complaints from the players that they weren't really seeing much of the country. Of course, they could hardly complain to Pew, who was fulfilling his part of the contract.

Gradually, as the marathon journey continued, the players became used to the conditions, and the daily routine of waking up and having breakfast on the train began to break down. As the train sped through the night to its next destination, the players stayed up late drinking, smoking, and playing cards in the buffet car, often missing breakfast entirely. When arriving at a town, the whole orchestra would disembark and have dinner at a local hotel or restaurant, to relieve the boredom of the buffet car. This did not always work, as on April 13th, a presidential primary election day, when the LSO found themselves in Pittsburgh. Charles Turner records in his diary:

> Don't expect many people tonight – the concert season is all over and we are doing rotten business. Have a bath at hotel, 25 cents. The big general election [sic] is on today and no liquor is

sold between one o'clock and nine. So we all have to be teetotal. We play at the Exposition Hall. Next place Cleveland. We get there some time in the night.

They arrived in the early hours, sober, slept for a few hours, had breakfast on the train, and made their way to Lake Erie despite the heavy rain. Turner admitted that by this point in the tour he wasn't really hungry and planned to miss lunch, three heavy meals a day being a bit too much for his constitution. However, he made up for it after an afternoon nap on the (stationary) train.

We can't get beer here only lager. Bass or Guinness can be had but it is 25 cents a bottle. All good scotch whiskies can be had 15 cents a time and you help yourself. Needless to say I take rather good nips and we get good value for our money in whisky. The pubs can stay open here as long as they like. Went and had the best dinner I have had. Here it is – Oysters. Soup. Salmon. Roast Lamb and green peas, orange punch, a beautiful kind of ice cream. Then a roast pigeon with potatoes, salad, asparagus, olives. Then another fine Ice Vanilla flavoured, and coffee. I went through the lot. We are getting fed fine. This was the best meal up to now, although they have all been very fine. I have not tasted tea since we left England. You can get it here but it is generally very poor. Concert in the Hippodrome, a very beautiful theatre – not filled as usual. Back on board the train and we start off at 1 am for Chicago. We are always travelling thro the night so we are not seeing much of the country. We have 345 miles to travel to Chicago.

Reading his description, it is hardly surprising that after three meals of that size, Turner found himself with a very small appetite, and the vast quantities of cheap alcohol that were consumed were gradually becoming a problem for some players.

As well as meals of gargantuan proportions, there were days when a quick stop-off at a local station buffet was the only form of sustenance. Unfortunately, the train was late on many occasions owing to unforeseen circumstances: a crack in one of the wheels, and probably leaves on the line. In the finest tradition of 'the show must go on', if the orchestra was late, it meant that there was no time to eat except by grabbing something from a passing station kiosk. If you've ever seen the present-day LSO in the rush for the teas at a rehearsal break, this account from violinist Wynn Reeves in 1912 will be familiar:

> As soon as the train stopped, I streaked across to the buffet seizing all I could see, removing glass covers in ten seconds, by which time the buffet was being mobbed. The proprietor came dashing out from behind the counter brandishing a revolver and shouted, 'I refuse to serve another thing until I know who is paying for this.' We looked at the counter which by this time was as stripped as if it had been attacked by a swarm of locusts. We assured the proprietor that Mr Fales the millionaire who was running the tour would pay and returned to the train. The loot for my party consisted of 4 sandwiches, 4 sticks of chocolate and a bottle of some mineral or other ...*

When they travelled to Montreal, the train was very late indeed, and consequently a fleet of lorries and extra manpower were enlisted to ferry the instruments to the hall. The concert eventually started nearly two hours late, but the audience was enthusiastic despite the delay. Whatever speed at which the gear could be taken to the venue, however, could not match the speed with which the orchestra descended on the station buffet. Having been trapped on a motionless train for hours with no food or drink, they again swarmed. Richard Tabb, a cellist, described the scene:

> Nikisch got in first. I've never seen him move so quickly. So scared was the buffet lady by the bearded Nikisch and his following horde that she, fearing the worst, swept the eatables from the counter and started to make her escape. Eventually

---

* *The LSO at 70: A history of the orchestra* by Maurice Pearton. London: Victor Gollancz, 1974.

order was restored, the players got half a bun each – the entire stock of the buffet.*

Whether because of the vast amounts of food being consumed, the equally vast amounts of alcohol, or just an orchestra getting used to being on tour, the critical response to 'the best orchestra in the world' gradually began to improve, as newspaper reviews attest. On reaching Washington, the players were presented to President Taft at the White House: Turner described him as 'an amiable, splendid gentleman, with a dignified and pleasant bearing'. Taft was only a few days away from a presidential election, and the hastily arranged meeting was undoubtedly part of his final push for re-election. His campaign failed, but the LSO received a great reception in Washington. Critics praised Nikisch and his orchestra for their brilliance, and special praise was given to the 'liquid beauty' of Miriam Timothy's harp. When the orchestra moved on to play in Detroit, the *Evening Statesman* rhapsodized about its influence on April 25th:

> On the tour they are making in the United States and Canada, they will have visited many cities, and every place they will have rendered richer for their visit. At the Armory in Detroit, an audience of upwards of 1500 people listened to this wonderful orchestra under the leadership of Nikisch, which proved a revelation of what orchestra playing can become. Whether Mr Nikisch could have produced so impressive an effect with an American orchestra might be debated. It is almost incredible that a hundred men could be moulded into a single instrument so delicately responsive as these men were. His ability in drawing from his men just exactly the shade of tone he wishes seems like magic.

Gradually, towns and critics were being won over, despite the occasional gripe, such as Turner complaining that 'the *Philadelphian*

---

* *London Symphony: Portrait of an Orchestra* by Hubert Foss and Noel Goodwin. London: Naldrett Press, 1954.

LSO players sightseeing in Washington, 1912.

Ledger gives the band good notice but says that the drums were irregularly walloped after the fashion of a rug beater'. (He did see the funny side, describing the review as providing the orchestra with 'much sport'.) In general, the tour continued to draw bigger audiences and better reviews. Morale on the train was high, and there is a sense in Turner's and Nisbet's diaries of the players beginning to enjoy themselves. Every now and then there was a tiny gap in the schedule, during which the players were able to see a little of America. On April 24th they arrived in Canada, and Turner describes the day as one of the best of his life:

> We first of all put our watches on one hour. Back to New York time. Wake about 7.30. Get ready and breakfast on train. Very fine and we wish we could always live on the train. While breakfasting the train stops at Niagara – and we view the Falls. Many get out and I finish quickly and get out also. You don't grasp the magnificence of the Falls from a distance. First of all we raid the souvenir shop and the money starts to fly. I spend

about $10 in no time. Take a train ride all round the Niagara loop. We pay 1 and a 1/2 dollars for the whole trip and worth it. We go underneath the Falls in oilskins. The ride round is very fine and we see the whole thing in real fine style. The best day we have had on the tour. I have my photo taken many times. Hope to get some. The weather is very beautiful and we are very lucky in fine weather. There is tons of ice near the Falls, which is just breaking away and going boiling down the river. We leave about 4 p.m. and take train for Buffalo. Not our own train, that had gone. Dress and dance. Usual train. Sleep. Leave about 9 a.m. next morning.

Perhaps the most vivid description he gives of a tourist excursion is to the Armour & Co. potted-meat factory:

We are off again, and arrive Chicago about 11 a.m. We sometimes do 80 miles an hour. Terrific travelling. Go to lunch at the Kuntz Remmel Hotel – rotten. Take a trip on the overhead train roads to 'Armour & Co', the great tinned and potted meat merchants. Get shown round the gigantic place. One hour and walk about a mile and half. See them killing pigs and cattle in great numbers and see the whole thing from the cattle in the yards to the beef in tins, etc., sausages, lard and all sorts. The best thing I have seen in America yet.

The confidence of the orchestra, and the mystique surrounding Nikisch, grew by the day. In every city they visited, admirers and (importantly) rich donors were entertained in the conductor's personal railway carriage, 'Signet', a carriage normally reserved for royalty. Like the handkerchief-waving women of New York, the ladies of other American cities seemed to be falling under his spell, as reported in the *Milwaukee Journal*:

Society women are said to have engaged all the choice seats for the London Symphony Orchestra concert because Arthur Nikisch conducted. When Milwaukeans, Saturday night, saw that marvellous left hand, fluttering in the air, pulsing like an

> incarnated heart beat gathering that orchestra unto him as
> though it were a mere extension of his own musical personal-
> ity, they wondered why those Boston women did not engage all
> the seats ...

One wonders what it is about conductors and their fluttering hands that makes them so attractive.

As is often the case, although things seemed rosy on the outside, the tensions behind the scenes sometimes spilled out backstage – and even, on a couple of occasions, on the stage. When playing in Chicago, a concert that was favourably reviewed, Turner, who has a high opinion of the maestro, tells us, 'Go to concert in the auditorium, another beautiful theatre and very big. Fine house, the best we have had. Mr Nikisch gives certain members the bird for inattention.'

Things remained tense for several days. When an orchestra tours a programme for more than a few days, there are moments when familiarity can breed contempt, concentration can lapse, and performances can suffer. There can be little doubt that playing the same pieces over and over again, while travelling in the way they did, caused the orchestra a few problems. A few days later, the LSO played to an all-female student audience at a university in Madison, Wisconsin. Sensibly, Howard Pew had arranged for them to be fed in the dormitory (which was empty of students), play the concert, and then leave on the train as quickly as possible before anyone could get into trouble. The double-bass section seem to have had trouble concentrating that afternoon. Whether it was the repetition of the repertoire, or the distraction from the fine young ladies of Madison, Nikisch wasn't happy again, but this time the orchestra didn't take it lying down:

> Play to a good house in the gymnasium. It stands on the shore of
> the lake, students must have a good time. A swimming bath in

the cellar fine. Rifles are stacked all round the walls. They are all evidently amateur soldiers. More trouble with Nick. He gets on the basses and gives them the bird. He gets the bird back.

Evidently, the bass section was enjoying the view, and nobody was going to stop that. It is interesting to note that Turner, who in his diary has previously referred to Nikisch as 'Maestro' or 'Mr. Nikisch', is by this point in the tour referring to him as 'Nick'.

The pressure of the tour, however, was gradually taking its toll. Alcohol consumption was on the rise, and rumours were rife that the leader, Arthur Payne, wasn't always fully in control of his bow arm – or his fingers. But the board managed to keep everything under wraps for the benefit of the sponsors regularly joining them on board the train.

Controlling the orchestra was one thing, but the conductor? That was a little more tricky. In one Midwestern town, one of the orchestra's many guarantors came storming backstage during an interval. She shouted at Pew and Busby that her financial support had been secured for the tour on the understanding that

LSO in Wichita, Kansas, 1912.

there was to be an orchestra of 100 people. She had been sitting watching the first half, and presumably counted that there were in fact fewer on stage. She wanted her money back. Whilst the management tried their best to calm the situation down, she continued shouting. Nikisch came out from his dressing room to see what the fuss was about and was given the details of the unimpressed sponsor's account. Nikisch fixed his eyes on her and said, 'Madam. If you do not continue your guarantee, I do not continue to conduct the concert.'

Whilst Pew and Busby stood holding their breath, the sponsor went quietly back to her seat. Nikisch completed the concert, but the strain was beginning to show. The final concerts in New York were looming ominously on the horizon.

15 FAME
2012

Michael Francis breaks a leg

Back from our whistle-stop tour of Lithuania and Russia where, yet again, I found myself watching a major sporting event featuring England (football) or Wales (rugby) on foreign soil. Last January, I scoured South Korea looking for a bar in which to watch the France v Wales rugby international, only to give up, go to bed, and find it on television in my room. This time, however, we hot-footed it off the plane and straight into the centre of Vilnius to find a suitable bar.

It wasn't long before we saw lots of open-mouthed men staring with beer in their hands, lit by the familiar flicker of a TV set. In we ploughed. o–o. Another vintage performance. It was, strangely, less stressful watching it with a Lithuanian commentary, as they didn't seem to get excited about anything – unlike the men in the bar. There were no national colours to be seen, so I assumed they were all locals, especially as we had been given the 'you're not from round here, are you?' look as we arrived. So imagine my surprise when we scored the first goal and the entire bar cheered and drank heavily: obviously English, I thought. I was baffled when Sweden scored, though, as the same people cheered just as loudly and drank just as heavily. I have imagined various possible explanations for this – you choose:

1. They were all football lovers, and cheered on both teams as a sporting gesture.

2. There is a high proportion of children from Anglo-Swede marriages living in Vilnius.

3. After the first England goal, they were all so drunk that they lost the ability to differentiate between colours, and so couldn't tell the difference between the teams.

In any case, we drew, which was good enough.

The concert the next day in Vilnius was fun, albeit nerve-racking to begin with, as Valery's plane was delayed. He was an hour late for the already late rehearsal. Lennie, the chairman, had called him earlier.

'Where are you?'

'I am here, Lennie!'

'I can't see you.'

'Look up!' His plane was circling somewhere above our heads.

It was decided that we should start without him: cue a big break for Mike Francis, one of our bass players, who is studying conducting. Mike prides himself on his suave skills, musical brain, and his proto-conductor wardrobe. At last, he stood in front of the LSO, hands poised; at last, we were going to be able to take the mickey out of him for ever.

Imagine my disappointment when, against all the odds, it turned out that he was good – especially as there were two newspaper critics at the rehearsal.* After initial giggling, everyone followed his beat, which doesn't always happen.

The next day we flew to St Petersburg, Valery's home. Going through customs took ages for some players, but not for me, as I play an instrument they couldn't care less about. I got straight through, while my string-playing friends had to wait for customs to count the strings on their instruments.

The concert started late, as the traffic was so bad, and by the time we got on stage (without our jackets) it was a sweaty 31 degrees. At the end of the concert there were puddles on the floor; it looked as if there had been a rainstorm in the hall. But it was a great show, and one that I will remember long after the clothes have dried out. It would have been nice to stay and look around, but we had a plane to catch as soon as we'd picked up a beer and a sandwich from Soviet Subway. This was a 22-hour day by the time I got home, and we were working again later that afternoon. So I crawled into bed at 2.30 a.m., and Mrs Davies turned over to face the wall. I smelled worse than I thought.

A half-awake voice said, 'Glad you got back safe, but you smell.'

Home sweet home.

Torque of the town

It looks like it's going to rain in Spain again. We are, at this very moment, sitting on a brand-new train travelling from Valladolid to Madrid, and there are dark storm clouds gathering on the horizon. Sue Mallet, once again, is prowling the corridor looking for victims to sign up for extra work. I have been reading through a few articles about the LSO in 1912 and the reviews from the concerts around North America, but a more recent piece caught

---

* Michael Francis has since left the LSO to pursue conducting. At the time of writing, he is chief conductor and artistic advisor, Norrköping Symphony Orchestra.

my eye last week. The journalist in question is no stranger to controversy, and I don't think this is the place to start a war of words, but: Jeremy Clarkson said that we were a 'tribute band' in his weekly rant in *The Sunday Times*. The way he sees it, because we play other people's music rather than original material, we are no different to bands who emulate their musical heroes by trying to sound exactly like them.

Of course, if Mr Clarkson were to come to an LSO concert – and he is most welcome – he wouldn't hear a faithful facsimile of the first performance of Brahms 1 (which we are playing tonight). He would hear one interpretation of Brahms. We also sound very different depending on who is conducting, and the LSO of 2012 sounds different to the orchestra of 1912. He might more justifiably have called us a 'covers band', as we do perform other people's material. But of course, just as in his popular motoring show – *Fifth Gear*, I believe – which my kids love, whatever he says is with tongue firmly in cheek.

This week, we are playing Sibelius 7 with Daniel Harding. This is a piece we have played quite a lot with Sir Colin, and yet the two conductors bring very different things to the same piece. Daniel has very clear and strong ideas about how he wants the music to sound, but even with the same ideas in his head, it would be a very different performance if he were standing in front of a different orchestra. I really like the way he shapes the Schumann Symphony No. 2: not a piece I know at all, but it has some great tunes, and Daniel has been getting us to lighten up a bit. We are also joined once again by Imogen Cooper, playing a Mozart concerto. She is such a joy to play with, it almost feels like playing in a chamber group, as she is constantly listening to the orchestra and reacting to things we do as well as the other way round. Every night, the performance is slightly different, but always a highlight of the concert for me.

Britain's got talent

As we left the country earlier this week, the news was dominated by an issue of world-shattering importance which took up more column inches than any other story. The headlines shouted from the free newspaper on the plane, and the clever columnists dissected the statistics and reached their own startling conclusions. Personally, I thought the right decision was made, and I look forward to next year's *X Factor* with huge anticipation.

I arrived early at Gatwick and went in search of breakfast upstairs, where I was greeted by a shouty man who, unfortunately, had been given a microphone to play with at 6.45 a.m. Everybody around him was trying to pretend they were still asleep, and he was shattering their illusions. Mine, too. I wandered past and sat down to have breakfast; his voice subsided into the background noise of teacups on saucers, the clink of china plates, and the ineffectual sawing of plastic cutlery.

When I came back out, a small crowd had gathered around this man and his ... well, his giant snow globe. It was a giant, inflatable one, very like the small versions that you shake to make it 'snow' – except this was too big to shake, although he was doing his best by shouting *really loudly*. I walked a little nearer and saw that it was a sort of karaoke booth: you could step inside the giant snow globe and belt out your favourite song while the proprietor bellowed encouragement at you. It was called 'Gatwick Factor'. I can't tell you how much I wish I was making this up.

Coming your way in 2015, subject to sponsorship:

Max Factor: Looking for Formula 1 talent (costumes optional)

Factor Factor: Quick-fire algebra quiz

XXXX Factor: Late-night drinking competition.

Tractor Factor: West Country talent show

Musicians are often described as having 'the X factor': Gergiev, for instance. I did a pre-concert interview with him in Warwick last week where we discussed, among other things, his batonless finger-shimmering technique. The question people ask me the most is: does a conductor make a difference to an orchestra, or could you just all do it yourself? The truthful answers are 'yes' and 'yes, sometimes'. Mahler 2 is always a piece that ignites something in your soul, no matter who is conducting, but when a great conductor is in charge, the piece is raised to another level. If you ask me, however, to explain *why* he is so great, the only explanation is that he has the *X Factor*. The same goes for players in the orchestra. There has recently been a new addition to the LSO flute section, which at last makes us complete: Adam Walker, 21, joined us this week. We had a lot of great players auditioning for us, but when Adam came in and played it was quite obvious that although he was young, he had something that others didn't. Again, let's call it the X factor.

Britain certainly has got talent: it just doesn't always enter the right competitions.

I'm a celebrity … get me out of here

The more I write about music, the less I have to say on the subject: describing the same concerts over and over again can get a little tedious. But then, all of a sudden, something quite unexpected happens and I have something new to write about. Yesterday was one of those days.

The first half of the concert in Tokyo consisted of Prokofiev's 4th Symphony (first version) and Second Violin Concerto (only version). Vadim Repin was the soloist. He got a thunderous reception for his interpretation, and was called back on many times; at last he came back on clutching some sheet music. This isn't

something I had seen before, and there was a very quick stage move as both the front desk of cellos and the leader, Andrew Haveron, swiftly put up their music stands for him. They were all so keen to help that he suddenly had two music stands for his piece.

It was at this point that Repin stood Andrew up as if he was introducing him, and they both stood up in front of the music. Just as most of us were looking at each other wondering if perhaps Andrew had been at the sake, the two of them launched into the second movement of the Prokofiev Sonata for Two Violins.

If you don't know it (and I didn't), it is a fast and very difficult piece, but they sounded as if they had been performing together for years. The audience and orchestra looked on in awe; it really was a highlight of the tour. At the reception, Andrew explained that Repin had suggested it the day before at a party they went to, and they had put it together earlier in the day. It's typical of his modesty that he felt the need to point out that he had played it once before; but I'm guessing that wasn't in front of an orchestra and audience in a major concert hall, with a famous international soloist. Simply breathtaking.

As we didn't have to get up early the next day, a group of us decided to try out another traditional Japanese leisure pursuit: karaoke. We headed up to Roppongi, which is a lot like Soho, and booked ourselves a room for 22 people – about 25 per cent of the orchestra. Earlier in the day, some of us had bumped into a guitarist from Britain who was also staying at our hotel. He was over here playing with pop star Craig David, 'and said that they would like to join us later. We were very excited about being joined by a 'proper' singer for our karaoke bash, so we all warmed up with a pre-performance drink, and started.

You'll recognize the pattern if you've ever been to karaoke before: at first nobody much wanted to sing, but by the end of the evening there was a queue. Every so often a ripple of excitement would go round the room: *Craig David has arrived!* But he didn't come; so we sang some of his songs instead. The duets were flowing as fast as the wine, and I even had a go myself. We all seemed to be getting typecast: I was made to sing 'Delilah', the unofficial Welsh national anthem. First violinist, Laurent Quenelle, sang 'La Vie en Rose' and Miriam Loeben sang '99 Luftballons'.

Craig David is here!

No, still not here: just his guitarist. Deep down, I knew he wasn't going to come, but we were having fun anyway. I stepped up to the mike for one last duet with Helen Edordu (percussion), who, because she is a lot younger than me, didn't know most of the songs that I knew. We eventually found that we both knew a Westlife song, for which I could only apologize. We were well under way, singing in harmony and everything, when I'm told that Craig David did actually appear in the foyer. Mike came running into the room shouting 'He's here! He's here!' over and over, like a twelve-year-old girl. We reached the climax of the song. Craig came into the back of the room and stood there, looking at the cream of the LSO in full flight.

Then he turned around and went home. He didn't even finish his drink.

As I laid my head on the pillow that night, I came to the conclusion that he was intimidated by my singing, and felt it better to leave than show himself up. Some people crumble when faced with greatness.

Thank goodness we had Andrew Haveron.

Is that the President?

I awoke in our Costa Mesa hotel with sun streaming through the curtains, and stumbled across my room to look out of the window. We had arrived and checked in at half past midnight, so when I went to bed I couldn't see anything, but now a glistening and inviting blue swimming pool was revealed. I went for a run, and then dived in. Any thoughts of sightseeing left my head.

When I finally made it back to my room, I could see an enormous traffic jam on the freeway. I asked the guy on the desk if it was usually this busy, and he told me that it was because Barack Obama was in town. Wow, I thought: we'd better play well, if we are to maintain the special relationship between our two countries. I hope he likes Prokofiev.

I ironed my shirt, polished my shoes, and made my way to the rehearsal. There was a buzz in the air, but, being a pro, I put aside thoughts of meeting the President and concentrated on the music. I had to negotiate through another Classical Symphony. Valery strode onto the stage in the fabulous hall with a big grin on his face. This is a bad sign for me, as it usually means it's going to be quick.

It was.

Just as the last movement started, he looked over at the woodwind and smiled. Oh, dear, and I hadn't fastened my safety belt. An additional *frisson* of tension (as if I need it) comes from the five page turns in the last movement. These all have four bars' rest to turn before the most difficult bits appear. So far, I have managed them, but I have a recurring nightmare that one day my music will fly off the stand. As we flew up onto the final six top Ds, Siobhan and I looked at each other and laughed, and then my hands started to shake. I think it's probably the same adrenaline rush bungee jumpers get.

When I came off stage, I hoped that the President would have been impressed, but I hadn't seen any massive security guards, so maybe he didn't make it. But what was this? A large group at the end of the green room, all laughing and joking with someone and shaking hands. Could it really be the President of the United States of America, come to see us?

No, actually, it wasn't; it was a leader of men in many respects, but not the President. It was our previous managing director, Sir Clive Gillinson. I joined the orchestra towards the end of his tenure, before he left to run Carnegie Hall in New York; but a lot of the way we work now is down to his leadership, and we certainly have a lot to thank him for. There were plenty of people who were far happier to see him than they would have been to see Barack Obama; no offence to the President, of course. In fact, when we are in Washington, I shall try to pop in and say hello. My parents' house is called 'Ty Gwyn', which is Welsh for White House. I find it's always good to have something in common as your conversation starter.

The LSO has left the building

The longer this tour lasts, the more I feel like a rock star. I should point out to my family at this early stage of my rambling metaphor that this does not extend to the sex and drugs cliché – although I did have some dessert wine last night in Budapest.

We played in Zagreb a couple of nights ago. It's a fantastically beautiful town which we sadly didn't have much time to look around. I realized only as I got my passport out again this morning that we are visiting seven countries in ten days, so there isn't much time for sightseeing. In Zagreb there is a beautiful theatre from the nineteenth century. We didn't play there. There is also a modern concert hall. We didn't play there, either. We played in the massive sports arena, which seats 10,000 people: not exactly intimate. We had a seating call, mainly to check microphones in the cavernous hall. Let's just say that Prokofiev 5 has never sounded so loud.

When you regularly play in some of the best halls in the world, the prospect of playing in a drafty arena isn't great. My feelings didn't change when we got there: the stage was tiny in the hall, with a big stack of speakers to pump out the music that we had so delicately honed and sculpted over the last few months. Oh, well.

Then something odd happened. I knew that Valery was quite well known and popular in this part of the world, but I was taken aback when I walked into the hall. People had been arriving for quite some time, and of course the concert started late because of the sheer size of the venue. I asked Sue if they had sold many tickets, and she informed me that it was sold out. I assumed she was being sarcastic. There was quite a noise coming from the hall, and as I stepped onto the platform with the rest of the band, I was greeted with the sound of ten thousand people applauding. I'm sure it must be one of the biggest audiences we've had – like selling out the Barbican more than four times.

As is often the case at times like this, the orchestra went from being a bit miserable to playing very well indeed, spurred on by the audience. After the encore, I wanted to shout 'Good night, Zagreb!' extremely loudly down a mike, and maybe destroy the drum kit; but I decided against it, and stayed on backstage, where the organizers of the concert provided us with beer and food.

I couldn't help notice, as well, that there were warning signs about what not to bring into the hall in Belgrade. These are standard, of course: don't bring drinks, cameras, or audio recorders – you know the kind of thing. This, however, was a picture notice: no dogs, shorts, guns, or flip-flops. How eclectic. How rock and roll: you can record the concert, but don't shoot anyone, especially not while wearing flip-flops.

Sunny Spoleto

Everything was going terribly well this morning. I had breakfast with Henrik from the Gothenburg Opera, who is playing second flute with us. We had time to catch up about student days in the palatial surroundings of the hotel in Palermo. We were discussing whether to have lunch beside the open-air pool when we reached Spoleto, or the nearby restaurant, when it happened: I bumped into our tour manager Mark Richardson.

'Bus leaves in five minutes, guys. Oh, and by the way, it's chucking it down in Spoleto.'

My perfect day of lounging by the pool, followed by a concert in the outdoors, was in doubt. I am going to have to word this very carefully, as I am of course totally committed to my job; but it did occur to me that if my outdoor lunch and swim were cancelled, there was the slightest chance that the same fate might befall the concert. Naturally, this would have been dreadful: a night off in a beautiful hotel in Umbria in July. Thank goodness I'd brought a book.

From that point on, the day went increasingly pear-shaped. We arrived at the hotel–spa–leisure complex (their description). My basic writing skills cannot do justice to the strange beige atmosphere that greeted us in the foyer, the lift doors that tried to kill you if you weren't quick enough, the crackling polyester bed-linen which had been used by the previous occupant, or the inexplicable tackiness of the carpet in my room (I refer both to its design and its keenness to liberate my flip-flops from my feet). I could tell you about the madwoman on the desk who was sending people to eat at the local pizzeria, a ten-minute walk away in torrential rain, which was in fact closed. Despite being told it was closed, she continued to send people there. We realized this must be some form of queuing system for the hotel restaurant (the two bars were closed). There were so many people trying to get in to have lunch that she was implementing a strategy to prevent the restaurant being overwhelmed.

The restaurant was overwhelmed.

We sat down and waited for menus, only to be told that there weren't any; you got what you were given. As a waiter approached the table with a large bucket and a ladle, several of us decided to make a break for freedom. We leapt on a bus going into Spoleto, a forty-minute drive away. The rain was getting harder.

Spoleto is a beautiful place, even in the rain. We saw the area where we were expecting to play: a stage in front of a pretty church, with the square and road sloping naturally upwards to make a raked seating area. It was a lovely sight – and completely water-logged, with no weather protection for the orchestra whatsoever.

Now, a few drips here and there are OK, but some of the stringed instruments in the LSO are worth a small fortune. Some players' bows alone are worth as much as a conductor's fee (if you can possibly imagine such a high figure), and that varnish isn't the same stuff you put on your fence to protect it from the rain. I was becoming even more concerned that we might be forced to have an evening off.

Sharon and I had lunch in a lovely little family restaurant with a few other friends, and the rain just kept on falling. Our meals included plenty of truffles, the local delicacy. We were seriously considering whether to ask what time they opened in the evening – as, quite clearly, the concert wasn't going to go ahead – when the clouds parted, it stopped raining, and the sun came out. You can imagine our relief.

The orchestra began arriving on coaches, and we tried not to look smug at having escaped an afternoon in the hotel. We all drifted down to the stage, which was covered in people drying the chairs. Our orchestral manager Carina McCourt was putting music on the stands, and extremely well-dressed Italians were drinking wine before the concert. The sunshade was in front of the stage to protect us from the now searing heat. We had our regulation clothes pegs to hold the music down, just in case it got windy; but there were no clouds in the sky, and we looked set for a lovely evening's music making. What could go wrong?

The concert started about fifteen minutes late, partly because everyone coming to the concert was so relaxed; and why not? Spoleto is one of the prettiest towns I've seen: tiny cobbled street, lots of nice places to sit outside and eat. They had an evening of beautiful music, followed by fireworks, to look forward to. Why rush? I should mention, by the way, that we were being filmed by Italian broadcasters RAI for a television programme, so we were under a little extra pressure. Hot lights, cameras on stage, and a swooping boom camera overhead were all extra distractions.

It's amazing how much noise an audience can make simply by sitting talking and moving around whilst we tune up. Often, it's not until everyone is totally silent and we are about to begin that we become aware of the ambient noises around us. This didn't really matter as Daniel strode onto the stage, turned to us, and launched into Strauss's *Don Juan*; all you could hear was the sound of the LSO reverberating off the ancient stone walls which surrounded us. Gradually the light levels began to drop, and Daniel returned to the stage to conduct Stravinsky's *Firebird*. If you don't know this piece, the first minutes are very quiet; played outside, they are almost inaudible. The Italian audience was incredibly attentive and quiet in seats that didn't look particularly comfy, being tipped forward down the hill and, I imagine, still a little damp from the earlier deluge.

When I used to live just off Guildford High Street many years ago, I would often be woken up – or indeed have my *alfresco* wine-drinking disturbed – by the local youth racing up and down on small scooters or souped-up cars, making a right racket. The young people of Spoleto were not to be seen anywhere, but the second we started playing very quietly, about thirty swifts began to swoop endlessly around the courtyard where we were playing. Their shrieks drowned out most of the first ten minutes of the *Firebird*, and the bird-like figurations from the woodwind in the second part whipped them into a frenzy over my head. I had one hand poised at my umbrella. I have heard that they throw vegetables sometimes in Italy, if they don't like a performance. I couldn't see the birds carrying any vegetables, but I'm sure they were armed, and I had only one set of tails. We scared them off with the Infernal Dance, but once again, in the very quiet horn solo at the end, David was drowned out by their shrieking. (As famous as he is, I'm sure it wasn't the first time.)

We had an interval of fifteen minutes, during which we all looked up at the sky, as by now the wind was picking up a bit and it was turning an ominous shade of black. Oh, well: the show must go on.

The second half began with a huge gust of wind as we played the opening of Brahms 2. I reached for my pegs and carried on. It's all right when you are a string player, as you have two players to a stand, so at least one of you keeps playing whilst the other puts pegs on everything. I am always left in a bit of a pickle. Take the first page-turn of the Brahms. It's pegged to the stand on the left- and right-hand sides. At the end of the right-hand page I have four bars to turn, always a bit tricky at this speed, but much worse when you have to undo two pegs. To make matters worse, on the next page is a solo; so I have to decide whether to sacrifice the last few bars of page one and peg down page two to play the solo, or play the last four bars of page one, turn and leave page two unpegged, thereby courting a possible wind-induced solo malfunction.

While I was making these important split-second decisions, there was a camera on a boom swinging over the second violins, coming straight at me for my solo. I was sitting on the edge of my chair, my flute on my lap, trying to peg down one side of music with the other peg in my mouth, looking like a right idiot. It should make compelling viewing when it's eventually broadcast.

Predictably, music and stands became separated by the wind during the first movement. You can always tell when this happens: someone, perhaps the first bassoon, suddenly stops playing, instead generating a frantic rustling of papers and, usually, a fair amount of swearing. We can but hope that there will be no subtitles on the televised version. In situations like this, there is very little you can do but laugh, shrug your shoulders, and carry on. We did so, until we reached the second movement.

I was fairly relaxed: I'd kept all my music on the stand, and there were no page-turns in this movement, so I had all four pegs on. The wind was whipping across the stage and ominous black clouds were racing across an ever-darkening sky. It all started well enough, but as we reached the halfway point, it began to rain. When this happens in Britain everyone gets their brollies out and we carry on playing under the all-weather canopy. Here there was no canopy, we were getting wet, and the rain was getting harder. Everybody was watching Lennie to see what we should do, and as quick as a flash, without stopping playing, Daniel continuing to conduct, they had a conversation which went something like this:

'It's raining!'

'Yes, I'd noticed!'

'Let's get off!'

'OK!'

It was the quickest negotiation on record in the turbulent history of the LSO. The last time I saw the orchestra get off stage with such speed was when they were offering us free beer in Cologne. Daniel Harding would have given Nikisch a run for his money in the race from that buffet car one hundred years ago! Of course there was little for us to do but stand under the arch and wait for the rain to pass, which took about fifteen minutes. We went back on to huge applause, the audience put away their umbrellas, and we started the second movement again. I am happy to report that the swifts had gone to bed and the rest of the concert went smoothly, although the entire woodwind section nearly missed the last section of the symphony when the oboe player made a basic outdoor concert error. In his relief to get to the last page before more rain, he forgot that he had pegged it down, and succeeded in ripping half the page off in a spectacular fashion. He then spent the rest of the piece trying to stop it being blown away. It kind of summed up the day, really.

Pizza, anyone?

Nearly home at last

We played a great *Firebird* last night in Dortmund. Valery always brings the world of the theatre right onto the concert platform. The music is brought into such sharp focus that I never feel the need for dancers to convey what is going on. When the music is happy, he looks happy and mischievous; when the music is angry, he looks like the last man in a bar you would pick a fight with.

A few of us were having a drink in the hotel bar last night, and Valery popped in and had a drink with us. This is not a regular occurrence for many conductors. As you can imagine, with his lifestyle being so very different from ours, it isn't always easy to find common topics of conversation. Valery is very happy to talk about football, but you do soon reach a barrier, as everyday life for him is not everyday life for us. Last night, we had this exchange:

Valery: '... I mean, Gareth, do you know how much a private jet across the Atlantic costs?'

Me: 'Er, not off-hand, no.'

That's a bit rock and roll for me. Inevitably, we got onto the subject of music, something we do all know about.

He was talking to Dominic Morgan, our contrabassoon player, describing how the music was supposed to sound in the *Firebird* when King Katchei wakes up. In the piece, two contra-bassoons growl around at a subterranean pitch I can only just hear, and gradually the two bassoons join; the pitch gradually gets higher and higher, to suggest him awakening.

Valery said that when we play it in the Proms later this year, it should be different.

'You know when in Africa they go out on the game reserves, and they have to shoot lions with tranquillizer darts? The lion falls down asleep, and then the vet can administer the medicine or whatever he needs to do. They have maybe half an hour before the lion starts to wake up. When he does start to wake up, he moves around ...'. He mimed a bad-tempered lion waking up after a heavy night at the oasis. '*Grrr ... rrrrr ...* finally he wakes up, and stands, and roars. That is how you should play it next time!'

He said all this with a smile on his face, but it does show you the kind of things that go on in his head to create the sounds he is after. Pure theatre. Somebody around the table suggested that to sound more realistic, the contrabassoons should have a couple of pints before the show.

Valery let out a roar of laughter. 'Oh, you would need at least eight pints, I should think!'

Eight pints before the Prom? Now that *is* rock and roll.

16 Bad News
1912

Touring such vast distances in cramped conditions took its toll on the players and conductor of the LSO, and being far from home brought its own challenges. Keeping in touch with family across the Atlantic was challenging. In the larger cities, players went to the bank to wire money to their families and post letters that took at least a week to reach home. Charles Turner had to wait two weeks before receiving his first letter from his wife.

Thoughts of distant families were surely very close to the surface on the cold morning in Wichita when the shocking news of the sinking of the *Titanic* first reached the players. Initial reports suggested that most people had been saved and help was on its way, but as the day progressed, the new became worse. Turner wrote, 'We hear about the White Star liner "*Titanic*" going down. It causes great concern.'

Thomas Busby might have reflected with his fellow board members, in the bar on board the train that night, on what might have been: something almost too terrible to contemplate. The players all knew that they would soon be making the return voyage on another ship, with their families waiting anxiously at home.

During a recent concert, one of the sponsors had spotted the smaller number of players on the stage. One of the reasons was that Joe Field, who had broken his knee on the journey over, was still back in New York in a nursing home; another was that violinist Wallace Sutcliffe had been ordered by doctors to rest up, owing to a strain on the heart. This meant that the orchestra had been playing two men down since the first week. Even Nikisch had been suffering with bronchitis for most of the trip. Getting plenty of rest, even when not playing, was difficult while travelling hundreds of miles a day, running to get food at station buffets and hotel restaurants, and then sleeping in narrow bunks. The pressure of life on the road began to take its toll on the group, and on one player in particular, as Turner recounts:

> Friday 26th April: Ottawa, Canada. The capital. This is where the beautiful parliamentary buildings are. Up early as usual and off to Russell House for breakfast. As we are taking the same – everybody is shocked to hear of Wallace Sutcliffe being found dead in his bunk. Dear old Wallace was one of my first dear friends in the LSO, and I had many talks with him on tour. Of course a general gloom was cast over the orchestra. I go to see poor Wallace in his coffin. I believe Fred Merry and I are the only two to see him.

Such was the pressure of their schedule that despite one of their number passing away during the night, the orchestra's rigid timetable was hardly affected. The funeral and burial of Wallace Sutcliffe took place at Beechwood Cemetery in Ottawa at 2.30 that same afternoon. The orchestra had a concert at 2 p.m., so none of his friends was able to attend, only the funeral directors themselves. With the LSO preparing to take the stage for

A GROUP FROM KING GEORGE'S PRIVATE ORCHESTRA

A Group from King George's Private Orchestra.

The private orchestra of the King, the existence of which is little known to the public, is composed of eighteen members of the London Symphony Orchestra. They are designated under royal warrant as "Musicians in Ordinary to the King." The picture opposite shows a group of them in court dress, and the medals worn by the members are personal decorations as follows: From Queen Victoria, Jubilee Medal; from King Edward, Coronation Medal; and from King George, Coronation Medal. The names of these members reading from left to right are as follows: W. A. Brennan, violin; W. H. Eayres, double bass; Edwin F. James, bassoon; Thomas R. Busby, French horn; W. M. Malsch, oboe; Wallace Sutcliffe, violin; Adolf Borsdorf, French horn.

All of these members accompany the London Symphony Orchestra on its American tour and will wear these royal medals at all of the concerts in this country. Miss Timothy, the harpist, is also a member of the King's private orchestra.

Members of the King's Private Orchestra, including Wallace Sutcliffe.

the matinee and his family as yet unaware of his death, Wallace Sutcliffe was laid to rest in section C, range 18, plot 15, in an unmarked grave. Unbelievably, the show really did go on that day. As the band left with heavy hearts for their second concert of the day, they received a telegram from the Mayor of Toronto: Sutcliffe's death was by now in the papers. It was of little comfort. Their train was delayed again and their evening concert in Montreal, in an enormous arena seating 23,000, started an hour and a half late.

Compounding the slightly surreal quality of the day, the orchestra was joined as soon as they began to play by thousands of birds which had been sheltering in the roof space and began to swoop down over the heads of the musicians, almost drowning them out completely. Maybe it was Sutcliffe looking down on them, protesting that they hadn't even been given the day off. Nikisch looked up at the birds and then proceeded to speed through the programme at a breakneck pace, no doubt much to the delight of the orchestra, who had probably had enough and just wanted to go home. After the concert, all the bars were shut, so they went back to the train to play cards, whereupon the train broke down again. Most definitely a day to forget.

17 The Show Must Go On
2012

In my seat

At the moment, I am sitting in your seat. That is to say, I am seated in the stalls of Avery Fisher Hall in New York City, watching the rehearsal of the Brahms Violin Concerto. I don't often get to watch my own orchestra; in fact, I don't often get to watch any orchestra these days, as we seem to be permanently on stage ourselves. I am seated about three-quarters of the way back, in the darkness that engulfs the rear of the auditorium. It is like a private concert, just for me.

Except, of course, I know from experience that it is nothing like the real thing; the orchestra is rehearsing, relaxed, a little jetlagged at the moment, but come the evening they will unleash everything they have left. During the concert, dressed in black and white and more than a few sparkles, the orchestra becomes one single force – no matter how tired or sad or unenthusiastic they feel, when the lights go down in the hall and up on stage, this group of people become the London Symphony Orchestra.

In the rehearsal today, however, what I see is not the LSO that you know. I see Tom and Malcolm, Sarah, Sharon, Gillianne, Chi, Chris, Joost, Alastair and 85 others I could name. I see my friends, not the orchestra. There are weeks when we spend so much time together that our disparate group of people becomes like a second family, with all its ups and downs, triumphs and failures. This is especially important when we travel around the world spending long periods away from our families back in London; we rely on the friendships formed in faraway places, on experiences shared both on and off the platform. When we welcome a new member, you can see them joining one of the many groups in the orchestra; they find their own way of doing things, they find their way to enjoy their time on tour, their way of coping with the madness of this lifestyle, and eventually it feels as if they have always been here. It takes a long time to find new members in this orchestra: we obviously want the best players, but it's more than that. They have to be part of it, they have to fit with the people too – and when they do, and it all clicks into place, it is wonderful.

Of course, things can't always stay the same. Players retire or move on to do other things. Recently, though, the orchestra has had to say goodbye to the much-missed Nigel Gomm, who lost his battle with cancer late last year. This morning, once again, the orchestra is hurting, as news filtered through to us as we wandered around New York that our principal oboe player, Kieron Moore, had passed away in the early hours of Sunday morning. Kieron had been receiving treatment for a rare form of cancer for the last few years and hadn't been able to play with the orchestra for some time – although we always kept his chair open for him to return whenever he could. Sadly it wasn't to be, and the atmosphere on the stage is one of shock and profound sadness.

I sat next to Kieron for the best part of a decade in the LSO, and formed a musical partnership the like of which I doubt I will find again. A gentle man, with a ruthless sense of humour and a sparkle in his eye, he was one of the greatest musicians I have ever worked with. As an orchestral oboist, in my opinion, he was without equal. He wasn't a flashy player. When a conductor stood him up to take a bow after performing yet another stunning solo, he would reluctantly rise from his chair and groan loudly, then sit back down again as quickly as possible; he didn't like a fuss. In an age of ever-increasing noise, where it sometimes seems that the louder you become and the more fuss you make, the more you are heard, Kieron was exactly the opposite. On stage he was quiet and contemplative, with a sound that could melt the hardest of hearts and an inner musical core that was so intense it took my breath away. When he played the famous solo from the second movement of the Brahms Violin Concerto, he did it with such fragility in his sound that the audience seemed to stop breathing for a while. Rather than outward showmanship, he could silence a room and draw you in to glimpse his musical soul. I can't begin to describe what a hole he has left in the orchestra.

One of his favourite cities was New York, and he left instructions for us all to enjoy ourselves and raise a glass to him, which of course we have. But now, the rehearsal continues for tonight's concert. The first movement is finished. There is a brief pause, and then the familiar sound of the second movement of the Brahms Violin Concerto begins. I see my friends look anywhere but at each other. Most people look at the floor, alone with their thoughts. And then the oboe melody starts. It is unbearable. I am glad to be sitting in the darkness at the back of the hall.

Maurice

The relentless schedule of touring with the LSO is tough. The hours are long and antisocial; families often take second place as we travel around the world; the pay isn't anything to write home about; and the moment your playing hits a bad patch or you are deemed past your sell-by date, there is a queue of young hotshots ready to take your place. The pressure of sitting in any chair in a top orchestra is huge, and if you sit in one of the 'hot seats' ... well, don't underestimate the peculiar combination of skills needed for one of those chairs. There is no hiding place on the stage when it all goes wrong.

You often hear the saying 'everyone has a book inside them', and it's probably similar with music, in that playing a particularly beautiful *Daphnis and Chloe* on the flute or a fabulous *Firebird* on the horn once in a concert isn't beyond most competent players. Once. But audiences want to feel something, they want to be moved – they want every concert they attend to be an event, something to talk about for years to come. Well, you do, don't you? If you go out to a concert on a cold, wet November evening and it is all present and correct but falls a bit flat because it's missing that elusive something, then you tend to go home feeling a little short-changed and disappointed. We players might all have one good performance in us; but the next day, when audiences have moved on from their evening out, we are typically on a bus or a plane or a train (or usually all of the above) moving to another city, country, or time zone, where we will try to reproduce the same thing again and again and again, night after night (if we are really fortunate, year after year). It is relentless.

I tell you this not to gain sympathy, but to emphasize the fact that every last member of the LSO on the stage every night is giving everything to the performance, because at that precise moment in time, it matters more than anything else.

This week we were all looking forward to a bit of light relief at a concert in Cologne, where we travelled for one day to play the music of John Williams, a composer best known for his film scores. His association with the orchestra goes back over 30 years. We played the usual favourites: *ET, Close Encounters, Raiders of the Lost Ark, Schindler's List,* and *Star Wars,* to name a few. There was special lighting, and there were clips of some of the films: classy stuff. Although this music is difficult in every section, it still allows us to let our hair down.

At the start of the rehearsal on Thursday morning it was announced that Maurice Murphy, our legendary principal trumpet for thirty years, had passed away in the night. A group of people who come together daily to make the most beautiful sounds in the world were stunned into silence for several minutes. The music stopped.

Although Maurice had retired for, I think, the third time in 2007, it felt as if he had never really left. His characteristic playing was as strong when he finally left as on his first day as principal in the LSO, when he rang out the top B flat of the main title of *Star Wars.* He was rightly famous for his stunning playing, with a name that commanded respect from the music-loving public, but to us he was so much more.

Everyone has a favourite story about Maurice: mine is a wonderful piece of advice, which is unprintable here. During a recording session a few years ago, we played through a new piece for the first time, and at the end there was a rousing trumpet finale in the style of John Williams. Maurice, Rod, Gerry, and Nigel dispatched it out somewhere into the stratosphere and, because we heard that kind of thing all the time, we took it for granted that that was what trumpets sounded like everywhere. They don't. After the run-through, the conductor and composer (who was American) punched the air and whooped, leaving us looking a little bemused, especially as it was a Sunday morning.

When he had regained his composure he looked across at the trumpets and paused, staring in disbelief.

'Oh ... my ... God ... Maurice Murphy? Maurice Murphy! I don't believe it! Maurice Murphy, playing my piece.'

We were all laughing by this point, partly because he pronounced *Maurice* to rhyme with *police*. It got worse when he walked across the studio, dropped to his knees, and held Maurice's hand, looking as if he was waiting to be anointed by the great man.

It was funny; but, to be honest, most of us understood how he felt. Many boys of my generation were obsessed with *Star Wars* as kids. To find myself, later on in life, sitting at Abbey Road with the LSO and John Williams recording the soundtracks for the new films, with the same man playing the same theme tune on the trumpet a few seats to my left, was astonishing. It's a memory I'll always cherish. Maurice was a musician who certainly did have one great performance in him – followed by another, and another, and another, until you just took it for granted that he was going to sound extraordinary. He kept up the highest of standards for over thirty years in the orchestra. To someone like me, knowing the punishing schedule we follow, that is awe-inspiring.

In many ways, it was only when he retired that it really dawned on us all how difficult it would be to replace him, and it's not surprising that it has taken someone fifty years younger than him to take over. When the orchestra has been travelling for two weeks and is in bad need of rest and familiar surroundings, it takes effort not to slip into playing on autopilot; but when Maurice put his instrument to his lips, be it for Mahler, film music, or a concerto, he could lift the orchestra single-handed.

The concert in Cologne, which we'd expected to be relaxed, if tricky, suddenly became the most important show we had done for some time. It was almost as if it had been planned especially. I must admit that I turned to look at the trumpet section more often than I normally do, because we all knew that they, above all, would find it a difficult night.

The sound of the LSO cut through the music more than usual that night. *Raiders of the Lost Ark* didn't sound as triumphal as it normally does, and *Schindler's List* was almost too much to bear. But as an interview with John Williams was played on the big screen, and he described the sound of that trumpet, we turned and launched into *Star Wars* with an energy I have never experienced in my life.

Maurice was our rallying cry, our talisman, and our friend. He may not be on stage with us any longer, but this week in the Philharmonie in Cologne, I could hear him loud and clear.

John Eliot is Unwell: a short play, based on true events

Scene 1: Backstage at the Salle Pleyel, Paris, France; five minutes before curtain. Sir John Eliot Gardiner, looking a little pale, is talking to principal flute player Gareth Davies.

JEG: How is your conducting, Gareth?

GD: Eh? Oh, well ... I conducted some students doing Beethoven 5 the other day, but it was just the wood-wind and brass. I'm no maestro!

JEG: Hmm, I see.

GD: Looking on the bright side, I could cue in the brass and woodwind and I'm sure the strings would be all right, there's loads of them! [*Laughs.*]

JEG: No, actually, I'm serious, I really don't feel very well. I'm not sure I'll make it through the concert. I might need you to take over.

Gareth exits stage left very quickly indeed.

Scene 2: *The conductor's dressing room, where a doctor is administering anti-sickness drugs to JEG. [This is a dramatic reconstruction of probable events, as I was still hiding.]*

JEG: Doctor, I need you to get me through the concert without me collapsing.

Doc: *Oui.*

JEG: Can you give an injection to prevent sickness which will enable me to conduct Beethoven 6?

Doc: *Oui.*

JEG: Thank goodness. I asked the flute player if he could conduct, and he seems to have disappeared.

Doc: *Oui. [Administers medicine.]*

JEG: *Merci,* Doctor. *Le spectacle doit continuer.*

Doc: *Oui.*

JEG and the doctor exit stage right.

Scene 3: *The auditorium. The orchestra has been waiting on the stage for nearly ten minutes, and the audience is restless. Where is John Eliot? When will the concert start?*

The door opens and John Eliot swoops onto the stage, bows, and turns to face the orchestra. He is obviously a little unsteady, but he raises himself up, dramatically pushes aside the stool provided, and gives a triumphant performance. He pauses merely to drink some water between movements, and then retires to his dressing room for the interval.

Scene 4: Just about to go on stage.

JEG: Ah, Gareth.

GD: Oh, hello, Maestro. I couldn't find you earlier. You look a bit better now, so I guess you won't need me after all.

JEG: Actually, I feel even worse. I'm not sure I'll make it through the whole symphony.

Gareth realizes that he is unable to turn around and disappear again, as he is now surrounded by violinists as well as viola player Malcolm Johnston.

Malcolm: All right, Gareth? You're lookin' a bit peaky yoursel'!

GD: Oh ... I'm fine ... fine, Malcy, really.

JEG: If I can't make it, I shall leave the stage, and Andrew will take over the performance.

GD: But who is going to play the clarinet?

JEG: No, you fool. Andrew Haveron, the guest leader.

GD: Of course.

Gareth is visibly relieved, and walks on stage with the rest of the orchestra. A marvellous performance of Beethoven 6 ensues and several hundred Parisians walk out into the chilly night, happy and unaware of the backstage drama.

Scene 5: John Eliot is standing at the stage exit, personally thanking each member of the orchestra. This is very nice as he looks as if he needs a lie down, and, to be honest, most conductors don't do this. Gareth approaches.

GD: Well done, John Eliot. You must be exhausted. Great show, though.

JEG: Thank you. Sharon, here, have my beer. I don't want it tonight.

Sharon: [*quickly takes beer*] Thanks.

GD: I actually feel disappointed.

JEG: Why's that, Gareth?

GD: I was looking forward to conducting tonight. I'd even thought about changing some of the bowings, and moving the basses further round to the side to enhance the harmonic range in this hall ...

JEG: Really?!

GD: Yes, I quite fancied making my debut in Paris.

JEG: Well, I'm still not 100 per cent. Maybe you'll have to conduct No. 9 tomorrow. Gareth ... Gareth!

Gareth quickly exits stage left. Sir John Eliot Gardiner sits down. Sharon drinks beer.

CURTAIN

The mussels in Brussels

Being ill on tour is uniquely distressing, and a player laid low by a virus or stomach bug is a player who needs to be replaced, often at short notice. On short European trips like this one, that isn't such a problem: as long as you have enough notice, a replacement can generally be found and flown out. But if we are far from home – say in Japan – we take two principals along in the wind and brass, illness cover being one of the reasons.

Sometimes, though, illness strikes at short notice and doesn't adhere to Musicians' Union rules, and there is no option but to struggle through a concert with gritted teeth (string players only) and concentrate on not throwing up.

I succumbed to an inconvenient bout of food poisoning myself a couple of years ago, and haven't touched shellfish since; in fact, it's making me a little queasy just to type this. Four of us had had a set menu at a lovely restaurant in Brussels that I have been to many times. The menu was a typical affair consisting of a salad, *moules marinières* and a chocolate mousse. I thoroughly enjoyed it.

Later on that afternoon, I made my way to the hall for a performance of Mahler 6 with Gergiev. It is quite normal on long tours to feel a little out of sorts, as we spend a vast amount of time flying, getting up early, going to bed late, eating late at night, and sometimes drinking a glass of wine after concerts. Living this sort of lifestyle can take its toll. Arriving at the hall, I felt a little tired, but nothing unusual; but gradually, during the rehearsal, I became hotter and hotter.

'It's hot in here, isn't it?' I said to Sharon.

'No, I'm a little chilly. You look a bit pale, actually,' she replied.

So after the rehearsal, I went outside to get a breath of fresh air. Come the concert, I was starting to feel a little off-colour. As luck would have it, I was playing the second piccolo part rather than the principal flute, and as I gradually started to go green, Sharon and I quickly flicked through my part looking for crucial moments for her to cover, should the worst happen. It took a while, but we found one bar. As we sat after tuning, Sharon turned to look at me.

'Are you OK? You really don't look very well at all.'

'I feel sick. Very sick, and a bit faint.'

'Maybe it'll pass as the concert starts. But if not, wait until a loud bit and go off stage.'

This made me feel a little better, as you never have to wait too long for a loud bit in Mahler 6. Having something to concentrate on and the physical actions of playing a wind instrument are often enough to focus the mind and stomach into postponing any ejections until after the concert. Sadly, I wasn't in the first movement of the symphony, so I sat for thirty-five minutes surfing increasingly intense waves of nausea. As Valery walked on to begin, Sharon reminded me, 'Just go off in a loud bit if you have to, and I'll cover you.'

I nodded, which was all I could manage. I don't remember much after that, except that it quickly became obvious I wasn't going to last the first movement without making an early exit. I kept hearing Sharon's voice in my head. I repeated her mantra, *just go in a loud bit, just go in a loud bit, just go in a loud bit,* and hoped I wouldn't take her advice too literally. As the music had now started, our conversation was restricted to a series of elaborate hand signals and knowing looks. I looked at her in panic, while she looked at me and wondered what shade of green Farrow & Ball would use to describe me. I indicated that I was going to leave shortly – she took my piccolo to save me weight and time. Every second counts.

There are moments in the life of an orchestral musician when nerves, technique, practice, and a little bit of magic come together, and a performance takes on a life of its own. You almost feel in total control of what is happening; an intoxicating feeling, at the best of times. On this occasion, for me, none of the above applied, and my body had other ideas. Wait for a loud bit? *I don't think so,* screamed my stomach as it rebelled. At possibly the quietest moment of the first movement, I stood up as gracefully as I could, bearing in mind I was feeling dizzy by now. I turned towards the basses, who, on seeing my impressive colour, parted like the Red Sea. There was a clear path of about fifteen feet between me and the door: I moved along it as gracefully as I could, as if walking off in the first ten minutes was normal, closed the door quietly behind me, turned, and ran as fast as I could, hand over mouth.

If you are familiar with Mahler 6, you will know that there are offstage cowbells. On this performance, they were moved into place once the orchestra had taken the stage. Their position was about five feet from the door I had just come through. Offstage cowbells are hung on a metal contraption which looks a bit like one of those temporary wardrobe rails that you hang your coat on at concerts. In my haste and dizzy state I hurtled at speed, in slippery concert shoes, towards the rack of cowbells. The percussionist wore a look of impotent horror as I clattered towards him. Fortunately, having mastered the scrum half side-step as a child, I felt adrenaline take over and leapt to the side, actually jumping *through* the metal wardrobe, and – crucially – under the cowbells. They didn't move. I carried on and made it to the bathroom – just.

With hindsight, it's a shame I didn't take the bells down in the quiet bit, as on retelling it might have been funnier; although not at the time. Cowbells make almost as much noise when you pick them back up as when you knock them over. From an artistic point of view, I am of course glad that my rugby skills came in so useful. After my first wave of sickness eased, I stood wondering whether to try and go back on; but every time I thought it would be all right, the Mahler swelled up from the stage and I began to feel nauseous. I am certain that this was a reaction to the mussels, rather than to Mahler.

It's not about the music

Last night we were in Cologne, one of my favourite German cities, with its beautiful cathedral, fabulous concert hall – and, of course, the free beer after the performance. We played the

Widmann Violin Concerto with Christian Tetzlaff: a great performance, and the composer, who was there, was very happy.

The second half was Mahler's 10th Symphony. He only ever finished the first movement, which is often played on its own. The rest of the piece was left in sketches and short score, and was finally pieced together in the 1960s by Deryck Cooke. It's a doom-laden work, with huge climaxes and some of the most sparsely textured, intimate music ever written for orchestra. Its cumulative effect is quite overwhelming. Daniel performed this piece with us about four years ago, and it was a performance that has stayed with me ever since. Without wishing to overdramatize, that night was a life-changing experience for me.

In July 2004, I was fortunate enough to be blessed with a daughter, who was adored by her two older brothers when she arrived. Two weeks later I was back in the same hospital, in a CT scanner, being diagnosed with testicular cancer. I'm sure there are many of you out there who have been through a similar experience. I went from the highest of highs to the depths of despair in a short space of time; the only good thing about it was that I had an excuse to sit down and cuddle my daughter.

This isn't the place for details, but it wasn't a time in my life I'd want to go through again. After an operation and chemotherapy I returned to work. I was a little battered, bruised, and groggy from the drugs, which often left me trailing off in midsentence, having lost my way at some point during a conversation. (Finally I was lost for words, something my friends were eternally grateful for.) I had managed to be ill during the summer holiday, so hadn't actually missed much work – I may be artistic but, boy, am I organized. I vividly remember that playing again in the orchestra was exhausting mentally and physically.

On my return, the first piece I played was Beethoven 9, a suitably life-affirming celebration. We were performing in the

City of London Festival at St Paul's Cathedral with Sir Colin. I can't tell you how happy I was to be sitting back in that chair, but something had changed inside me, and I didn't know what to do about it. I had always been an instinctive player rather than an analytical one. This has its advantages, but when something goes wrong, usually technically, it's not always easy to know how to fix it.

There are moments when the music surges forward and you feel excitement as a listener; hugely emotional moments, when a shiver goes up your spine. Those are the moments that are intensified beyond description when you are actually involved in playing the piece. Those are the moments that make this job the best job in the world. That night, after the show, Sharon kindly drove me to Waterloo Station. She could see that I was exhausted. I got on the train feeling very low: something wasn't the same as it had been. I simply hadn't felt anything during the concert – it felt as if I was going through the motions. It might have sounded fine, but I hadn't enjoyed it, simple as that.

This continued for a few weeks. I was sitting in one of the best seats in the house at the centre of one of the greatest orchestras in the world, and I felt nothing. I can remember speaking about it to friends, who reassured me that it sounded fine, but 'fine' in this band isn't enough. I spoke to my wife, and seriously considered putting my flute in its box and walking away.

Then one night before Christmas, after a couple of days of rehearsal, we came to the performance of Mahler 10 with Daniel. You don't need to read the programme notes to know that Mahler's obsession with death – particularly his own death – is never far below the surface. There is a particularly poignant moment at the start of the last movement where the texture changes so dramatically that it is as if the orchestra is inhabiting a different world altogether. The dull thud of a bass drum, possibly a slowing heartbeat, or a drum announcing a funeral procession, and then the deep, threatening rising scale on the tuba. Another dull thud. And silence.

This continues until we reach a strange chord procession, and then a simple flute solo. In the score it is marked *piano semplice* – quietly and simply. It is a beautiful tune that wends its way around a quiet string section, who change to chords that never quite go where you expect them to. It is deeply unsettling, eerily beautiful, and heartbreaking, all at the same time: possibly one of the most stunning pieces of music for the orchestral flautist in the repertoire.

In the concert, we worked our way through the piece until that first funereal thud. My heartbeat increased as the solo grew closer, but this time it felt different from the preceding weeks. As the tuba plodded away and the drum became more insistent, I could sense something in the music that exactly mirrored my state of mind. This doesn't happen very often, but when it does it is all-consuming, intoxicating. Daniel looked across the orchestra and cued me in: I closed my eyes, and played.

It's difficult to describe how it felt. Time seemed to stop; a wave swept across me, something that I had not felt in a concert for months. That night, and that piece, changed something in me. I opened my eyes again towards the end to make sure we were all in the same place, and it was over. I really have no idea whether anybody else heard anything different, and that really isn't the point; this was something personal to me. The music of Mahler flicked a switch somewhere in my brain. I spoke to Dan about it over a year later, and explained to him how I had felt. We were both aware of it in last night's performance; he just smiled, and we each knew what the other was thinking. Four years on, I find it terrifying, painful, and wonderful to play the piece, all at the same time.

We work, play, and tour together in this orchestra on a never-ending journey. We are, in many ways, like a big family. I am so lucky to have a job like this, and the opportunity to express something that words cannot describe. But we all have to remember, from time to time, that it's not always just about the music.

18 Almost There
1912

Towards the end of their tour the orchestra stopped off in Providence, Rhode Island, the home of Mr Warren Fales.

Fales, who had essentially paid for the entire trip, was looking forward to welcoming 'his' orchestra and favourite conductor to his home town, and had laid on a welcome like no other. Having grown used to slipping in and out of towns anonymously on their train, the LSO arrived in Providence to find the man himself waiting for them on the station platform, conducting his American Brass Band. Charles Turner wrote, 'Off to Providence. This is the home of Mr Fales and his fine band. Meet us at the station playing *The King* as the train arrives. It then plays us through the town to the hotel.'

Residents of Providence looked on in bemusement as a group of smartly dressed Englishmen were led up the main street by a brass band playing the British national anthem. As they reached the hall, Fales waited on the steps to greet Arthur Nikisch. The maestro approached, and Fales thrust out a hand in welcome. Nikisch was so excited that he dispensed with the normal pleasantries and showed his European roots: grabbing hold of the ample Fales, he hugged and kissed him several times on both cheeks. I imagine many of the ladies of Providence were envious. As Fales pulled away, slightly flustered, he said, 'Well, Nikisch, I'm glad to see you; but I don't know that I am glad as all that!'

The concert was a great success, and after much merrymaking the orchestra got back on the train to New York, the end of the tour firmly in its sights. The players were in high spirits, some more than most. At many points on the trip they had found themselves in 'dry' towns, where no alcohol was sold, but on this last train journey there was definitely an end-of-term feeling, with most of the orchestra staying up until the early hours. Charles Turner seems to have enjoyed himself, but nobody had a better time than Arthur Payne, the leader of the orchestra. He had been 'enjoying' himself rather too much on the journeys between concerts, and had been swaying rather alarmingly on stage. When they returned that evening, he caused a disturbance by drinking too much and then trying to wake up Warren Fales in the middle of the night by banging on the door of his carriage. When he sobered up in the morning, he apologized, and Fales accepted the incident as end-of-tour high jinks: the board of the orchestra, though, was unimpressed.

So acclaimed was the orchestra at this point that an extra concert had been hastily planned for the following afternoon in New York, this time at the Metropolitan Opera House. The opera singer Elena Gerhardt was to sing Strauss. Howard Pew had printed special flyers to advertise the concert to a hungry public, hoping to squeeze every last dime out of the orchestra's appearances. Rather tastelessly, he had advertised it as being 'made possible by the fact that the sailing of the steamer which was to take the Orchestra back to England was cancelled and the booking transferred to April 30th'.

Pew was never a man to miss an opportunity. Was the cancellation he mentioned a reference to the *Titanic*, its return voyage now obviously 'cancelled'? Perhaps; or maybe, in the aftermath of the disaster, the regular timetable was interrupted. We'll never know, but Pew took full advantage of the situation, and didn't allow the orchestra a free day to enjoy the city.

The response to the final two concerts in New York City was a far cry from that at the start of the tour. Newspapers gave fabulous reviews. Turner, however, was still suffering from unsympathetic listeners. A *New York Tribune* review of the Met concert was less than complimentary about the sound quality: 'The forcing into prominence of a pair of tympani which sounded in the conditions much like a pair of tin washboilers ...'. Fortunately, the same reviewer concluded the next night at the Carnegie Hall concert that, 'It was assuredly not the orchestra but the auditorium which was then responsible for the extremely dull and uninteresting quality of tone, the disturbed balance and the sudden incursion of the tympani into the realm of the tinsmith.'

Before the final concert in the far superior acoustic of Carnegie Hall, Nikisch put the orchestra through its paces one last time. Journalist Nixola Greeley-Smith from the *Pittsburgh Press*, who had come to interview him, found the rehearsal running over time and quietly took her seat in the hall to watch the great maestro rehearse. She described him as the most temperamental human being she had ever seen. The rehearsal was drawing to a close, the orchestra exhausted.

> 'More Fire! More Blood! Give me blood! Gentlemen, we are all a little tired, I know, but I must have blood. Three fortissimo notes – TA TA TAAAH!'

During Meistersingers the conductor did everything but stand on his head, and he made the orchestra do everything

METROPOLITAN OPERA HOUSE
Sunday Evening, April 28th, 1912

Mr. Arthur Nikisch
AND
The London Symphony Orchestra
MISS ELENA GERHARDT, Soloist

AMERICAN MANAGEMENT

MR. HOWARD PEW	MR. WARREN R. FALES
121 WEST 42ND STREET, NEW YORK	803-804 UNION TRUST BUILDING PROVIDENCE, R. I.

Program

OVERTURE---"Rienzi,"...WAGNER
SONG---"Der Widerspaenstigen Zaehmung,"............................GOETZ
           with Orchestral Accompaniment.
SYMPHONY in C Minor, No. 5....................................BEETHOVEN
    I. Allegro con brio.
    II. Andante con moto---A flat.
    III. Allegro---C minor.
PRELUDE, "Parsifal,"..WAGNER
SIEGFRIED'S DEATH MARCH---"Goetterdaemmerung,".........WAGNER
SONGS { "Ruhe, meine Seele," ....
        "Staendchen," ....
        "Morgen," .... } ....STRAUSS
        "Wiegenlied," ....
          with Piano Accompaniment.
VENUSBERG BACCHANALE---"Tannhaeuser,".....................WAGNER
OVERTURE---"Die Meistersinger," ....WAGNER

THE OFFICIAL PIANO OF THE LONDON SYMPHONY ORCHESTRA IS THE STEINWAY

LAST NIKISCH CONCERT
CARNEGIE HALL
Monday (Tomorrow) Afternoon, April 29, at 2.30
Program

OVERTURE,---"Oberon," ....WEBER
SYMPHONY in E Minor, No. 5...............................TSCHAIKOWSKY
SYMPHONIC POEM---, "Don Juan,"................................STRAUSS
HUNGARIAN RHAPSODY No. 1, in F.................................LISZT

Prices: $1.50 to $3.00. Box seats $4.00. Seats at Carnegie Hall.

THE OFFICIAL PIANO OF THE LONDON SYMPHONY ORCHESTRA IS THE STEINWAY

Poster for the final concerts at the Met and Carnegie Hall, April 1912.

but stand on its head – all with a singularly long and slender baton that whipped through the air like a death-dealing rapier in the riot music, but lured the love motif as gently as if it were a spray of apple blossoms fluttered by the south winds. He frequently stops the orchestra with an impatient tap on the empty stand – blood and fire was accompanied by a furious stamping of feet which suggested an army with banners of war coming. When he finally got what he wanted he curtly said, 'Thank you, gentlemen', and the rehearsal was over.

Nikisch wanted to go out with a bang, possibly to ensure future engagements, and also to prove the worth of his new orchestra after a shaky start. Turner wrote:

> We play the last concert in Carnegie Hall. The papers are commencing to rave about us and we get terrific notices. Anyhow, the big job is now finished and we have the night to ourselves in New York. Pass it very lazily with Fred Merry, have the usual nightcaps and off to bed. Many of the chaps feeling rather elated.

The New York Times was impressed, describing the overture as

> ... a capital performance, and it was succeeded by a still more striking interpretation of the fifth symphony of the Russian Wizard Tchaikovsky. Mr Nikisch's reading had so many points of significance that they cannot be adequately discussed in the passing record of a morning after ... the Strauss composition was performed with great brilliancy and aroused much enthusiasm. Altogether this was one of the best concerts given here by the London players and it ought to leave most delightful memories of them in the minds of local music lovers.

The New York Times commented that 'one of the players once said that Nikisch made them '"boil over with enthusiasm". He certainly did so last night.'

The concert was a triumph. The terrible notices of Boston were forgotten, and the LSO's billing as 'the greatest orchestra in the world' began to seem more plausible. At the end of the concert women charged towards the stage waving their handkerchiefs at Nikisch, causing great amusement in the orchestra as well as column inches for the tabloids. There was no doubt that the LSO had finally won American audiences over. (Such was the success of the tour that, immediately afterwards, Howard Pew invited the orchestra to return the following year. This was discussed at length, and a date pencilled in the diary for March 1914; but funding problems delayed it, and events in Europe then led to the outbreak of World War I, which would prevent the return of the London Symphony Orchestra for many years.)

Nikisch stayed on for a few days, but the orchestra had to get back to London to fulfil engagements, and the King wanted his band back. The morning after the final night, a very groggy orchestra awoke early and boarded the steamer *Potsdam*, a smaller ship than the *Baltic* from the outward journey. Cellist Joe Field was wheeled from the hospital with his leg still in plaster, having not played at all during the tour, and the personal effects of Wallace Sutcliffe were packed up to give to his wife on their return.

The journey home was fortunately uneventful, although the weather was very rough and meant that all the passengers were locked below decks for several days. As they passed through the ice in the fog, Turner commented on how slowly they were travelling, with the hooter sounding frequently keeping them all awake; but with the wreckage of the *Titanic* somewhere beneath them, nobody wanted to take any chances.

On board the *Potsdam*, the LSO board met to discuss the tour and the invitation to return. They decided that they would like to repeat the visit, but possibly with more money, fewer concerts, and less time spent on a train. Some nameless member suggested that the board should ask poor Mrs Sutcliffe to pay for the funeral of her husband, which she couldn't attend, and for the grave, which she would probably never see. Thankfully,

LSO players on the journey home aboard the *Potsdam*.

in an extraordinary general meeting a week later in London, it was unanimously decided not only to cover the costs but also to ensure that Mrs Sutcliffe received fees for all of the concerts on the tour.

Joe Field spent more time in a London hospital, and sued the White Star Line for damages; no doubt he joined a very long queue indeed. In the meantime, the LSO paid for his treatment, and he also received the fees he would have earned on the understanding that if he was successful in his legal action, he would reimburse the orchestra.

Arthur Payne and his erratic leadership of the orchestra had not been looked on kindly by the board, particularly after the drunken incident with Fales on board the train. On the journey home, they demanded his resignation. He again apologized for the incident, but refused to resign. When the board met again a week later, they wrote him another letter describing how, 'having freely taken intoxicants at or before many concerts, he appeared in a very undignified condition on the concert platform, thereby bringing his position into ridicule in the eyes of the members of the orchestra and the audience'.

They insisted on his resignation, and received it shortly afterwards, leaving W. H. Reed to step up to the chair, a position he filled for 23 years.

Finally, on May 10th, 1912, the ship passed Eddystone Lighthouse and the passengers saw Plymouth from the tender taking them ashore. Turner describes the scene:

> We watch the *Potsdam* steam out of sight from the tender and pass a fleet of destroyers steaming out of Plymouth Harbour. Soon pass thro' customs. Small trouble. Send wire and are on train for London at 9.30. England looks like a beautiful garden after what we have seen. Arrive safely in Paddington 2.15 p.m. Glad to get home after travelling perhaps over 12,000 miles in 6 weeks and 1 day.

After the tour, one of the first concerts for which the orchestra assembled was the *Titanic* Survivors' Memorial Concert, along with most of the other London orchestras. The orchestra gradually took back its place at the heart of the London music scene, and its relationship with Edward Elgar blossomed under its new leader.

Even though its return trip to the USA was delayed for so long by the outbreak of war, the relationship between the LSO and America has developed from its shaky start into a longstanding friendship. The 1912 tour was the only time the orchestra travelled to America by sea; in fact, the American people had to wait until 1964 to welcome the LSO again.

At the time of writing, the orchestra has visited America fifty-one times, with more trips planned in the future. It is quicker to get there these days, although sometimes the visa queues in

The last picture before steaming into Plymouth.

the embassy in London feel longer than that 1912 journey on the *Potsdam*. We now have our own conductor with mesmeric eyes, although I personally haven't witnessed the ladies of New York racing towards the stage at the end of concerts – yet. There are, however, many more women in the orchestra than the pioneering Miriam Timothy of one hundred years ago. Apart from the mode of transport and the moustaches, little has changed in the world of the LSO on tour when it comes to the practicalities. Long hours, cramped conditions, almost intolerable working hours: and yet, sitting on the stage in New York as the audience applauds at the end of the show, it's easy to remember the words of the *Evening Post* in 1912: 'They will surely never forget the warm welcome accorded them in the New World.'

fine

London Symphony Orchestra

1912 London Symphony Orchestra

First Violins

    Arthur W. Payne (Principal)

    W. H. Reed (Sub-Principal)

    H. Bonarius

    J. W. Breeden

    J. Bridge

    E. Carwardine

    H. Freeman

    J. W. Gaggs

    R. Gray

    C. S. Greenhead

    E. Lardner

    Philip Lewis

    E. A. Maney

    H. W. Reeves

    W. Sutton

    E. R. Wilby

Second Violins

    W. H. Eayres (Principal)

    W. A. Brennan

    R. Carrodus

    E. E. Halfpenny

    E. H. Hann

    W. Hann

    C. Hayes

    T. A. Kelley

    C. Newton

    C. B. Parker

    J. Ricketts

    A. Solomon

    F. Stewart

    W. Sutcliffe

    J. Wilby

    C. J. Woodhouse

Violas

    E. Yonge (Principal)

    V. Addison

    J. Cruft

    A. Dyson

    G. Goom

    T. Lawrence

    A. McLoughlin

    D. Reggell

    A. Wright

    H. Wyand

    A. Ballin

    C. Dorling

Cellos

B. P. Parker (Principal)
C. G. Blackford
J. H. Callcott
C. A. Crabb
J. Field
C. Goodhead
W. Hatton
J. E. Hambleton
W. Hobday
A. Maney
R. V. Tabb
J. Carrodus

Double Basses

C. Winterbottom (Principal)
F. Clement
E. Cruft
N. Morel
W. Silvester
W. H. Stewart
W. R. Streather
W. A. Sutch
E. W. Whitmore
C. Stewart

Flutes

G. Ackroyd (Principal)
H. D. Nisbet
J. Wilcocke
G. Slight

Piccolos

J. Wilcocke

Oboes

W. M. Malsch (Principal)
E. W. Davies
J. L. Fonteyne
E. C. Horton

Cor Anglais

J. L. Fonteyne

Clarinets

M. Gomez (Principal)
O. Hill
A. Augarde
A. Anderson

Bass Clarinet

A. Augarde

Bassoons

E. F. James (Principal)
A. Alexandra
J. Groves

Contrabassoon

J. Groves

Horns

> A. Borsdorf (1st Principal)
>
> H. Van der Meerschen
>
> T. R. Busby (2nd Principal)
>
> A. Brain
>
> G. A. Bennett
>
> A. Gaggs

Trombones

> Jesse Stamp (Principal)
>
> E. T. Garvin
>
> P. Jones

Tuba

> H. Barlow

Timpani

> C. Turner

Side Drum & Glock

> J. Schroeder

Bass Drum, Cymbals, etc.

> F. Merry
>
> A. White

Harp

> Miss M. Timothy

Librarian

> J. Schroeder

Orchestral Attendant

> G. Newman

2012 London Symphony Orchestra

First Violins

Gordan Nikolitch (Leader)
Roman Simovic (Leader)
Carmine Lauri (Co-Leader)
Tomo Keller (Assistant Leader)
Lennox Mackenzie (Sub-Leader)

Nigel Broadbent
Ginette Decuyper
Jörg Hammann
Maxine Kwok-Adams
Claire Parfitt
Elizabeth Pigram
Laurent Quenelle
Harriet Rayfield
Colin Renwick
Ian Rhodes
Sylvain Vasseur
Rhys Watkins
David Worswick

Second Violins

David Alberman (Principal)
Evgeny Grach (Principal)
Tom Norris (Co-Principal)
Sarah Quinn (Sub-Principal)
Miya Väisänen

David Ballesteros
Richard Blayden
Matthew Gardner
Belinda McFarlane
Iwona Muszynska
Philip Nolte
Andrew Pollock
Paul Robson
Louise Shackelton

Violas

Paul Silverthorne (Principal)
Edward Vanderspar
  (Principal)
Gillianne Haddow
  (Co-Principal)
Malcolm Johnston
  (Sub-Principal)
Regina Beukes
German Clavijo
Lander Echevarria
Anna Green
Richard Holttum
Robert Turner
Heather Wallington
Jonathan Welch
Natasha Wright

Cellos

Rebecca Gilliver (Principal)
Tim Hugh (Principal)
Alastair Blayden
(Sub-Principal)
Jennifer Brown
Mary Bergin
Noel Bradshaw
Daniel Gardner
Hilary Jones
Minat Lyons
Amanda Truelove

Double Basses

Rinat Ibragimov (Principal)
Colin Paris (Co-Principal)
Nicholas Worters
(Sub-Principal)
Patrick Laurence
Matthew Gibson
Tom Goodman
Jani Pensola

*String section players are listed
alphabetically and rotate within
the sections*

Flutes

Gareth Davies (Principal)
Adam Walker (Principal)
Siobhan Grealy

Piccolo

Sharon Williams (Principal)

Oboes

Kieron Moore

Cor Anglais

Christine Pendrill (Principal)

Clarinets

Andrew Marriner (Principal)
Chris Richards (Principal)
Chi-Yu Mo

E flat Clarinet

Chi-Yu Mo (Principal)

Bass Clarinet

Lorenzo Iosco (Principal)

Bassoons

Rachel Gough (Principal)
Joost Bosdijk

Contrabassoon

Dominic Morgan (Principal)

Horns

Timothy Jones (Principal)
David Pyatt (Principal)
Angela Barnes
Jonathan Lipton

Trumpets
Philip Cobb (Principal)
Rod Franks (Principal)
Gerald Ruddock

Trombones
Dudley Bright (Principal)
James Maynard

Bass Trombone
Paul Milner (Principal)

Tuba
Patrick Harrild (Principal)

Timpani
Nigel Thomas (Principal)
Antoine Bedewi (Co-Principal)

Percussion
Neil Percy (Principal)
Sam Walton (Co-Principal)
David Jackson

Harps
Bryn Lewis (Principal)
Karen Vaughan (Co-Principal)

Keyboard
John Alley (Principal)

London Symphony Orchestra, Conducted by Arthur Nikisch, Tour to USA and Canada 1912

ITINERARY

April 8		New York, Carnegie Hall	Programme 1
April 9		Boston, Symphony Hall	Programme 1
April 10		New York, Carnegie Hall	Programme 2
April 11		Philadelphia, Metropolitan House	Programme 4
April 12	(mat)	Washington, DC	Programme 3
April 12	(eve)	Baltimore, Lyric Theater	Programme 2
April 13		Pittsburgh, Exposition Music Hall	Programme 3
April 14		Cleveland, Hippodrome	Programme 2
April 15		Chicago, Auditorium	Programme 1
April 16		St Louis, Coliseum	Programme 2
April 17		Kansas City, Convention Hall	Programme 5
April 18		Wichita, New Forum	Programme 3
April 19	(mat)	Des Moines, Coliseum	Programme 3
April 19	(eve)	Des Moines, Coliseum	Programme 1
April 20	(mat)	Madison, University of Wisconsin	Programme 3
April 20	(eve)	Milwaukee, Auditorium	Programme 2
April 21	(mat)	Chicago, Auditorium	Programme 2
April 22	(mat)	Oxford, Ohio, Miami University	Programme 3
April 22	(eve)	Cincinnati, Emery Auditorium	Programme 1

April 23	(mat)	Toledo, The Valentine	Programme 1
April 23	(eve)	Detroit, Light Guard Armory	Programme 2
April 24		Buffalo, Convention Hall	Programme 2
April 25		Toronto, Massey Hall	Programme 4
April 26	(mat)	Ottawa, Russell Theater	Programme 3
April 26	(eve)	Montreal, Arena	Programme 2
April 27	(mat)	Boston, Symphony Hall	Programme 2
April 27	(eve)	Providence, Infantry Hall	Programme 3
April 28		New York, Metropolitan Opera House	Special programme with Elena Gerhardt
April 29		New York, Carnegie Hall	Special programme

PROGRAMMES

Programme 1

Beethoven	Overture, Leonora No. 3
Brahms	Symphony No. 1
Tchaikovsky	Symphonic Poem: Francesca da Rimini
Wagner	Overture, Tannhäuser

Programme 2

Beethoven	Overture, Egmont
Tchaikovsky	Symphony No. 6
Wagner	Prelude and Liebestod from Tristan & Isolde
Wagner	Waldweben from Siegfried
Wagner	Overture, Meistersinger

Programme 3

Weber	Overture, Oberon
Beethoven	Symphony No. 5
Wagner	Overture, Flying Dutchman
Strauss	Don Juan
Liszt	Hungarian Rhapsody No. 1

Programme 4

Beethoven	Overture, Leonora No. 3
Tchaikovsky	Symphony No. 6
Wagner	Prelude and Liebestod from Tristan & Isolde
Wagner	Waldweben from Siegfried
Wagner	Overture Tannhäuser

Programme 5

Beethoven	Overture, Leonora No. 3
Tchaikovsky	Symphony No. 6
Wagner	Prelude and Liebestod from Tristan & Isolde
Strauss	Don Juan
Liszt	Hungarian Rhapsody No. 1

Acknowledgements

There are many people who have helped me write this book. I firstly have to thank my wife, Michaela, and our children, who somehow put up with my need to play music and write about it; nothing in my life would be possible without them.

Thanks are due to the archivist at the LSO, Libby Rice, for mentioning Charles Turner's diary in passing which started the whole idea, and for the constant stream of information she provided; Digital Marketing Manager Jo Johnson for putting the pen in my hand, keeping it there when I'd had enough and for being my first editor; Sue Mallet for being such a good sport; Sharon, Sarah and Gillianne for being steadfast in the darkness of chapter 17; Nicky Holland; Norman Lebrecht and Tom Service for the encouragement of professional writers; Rob Hudson, Gino Francesconi and Clive Gillinson at Carnegie Hall; and Kathryn MacDowell and Karen Cardy for agreeing without hesitation when this book was born. Thanks also to Roberta Gagliani and Jack Nisbet for allowing me access their grandfather's diaries.

Thank you to Olivia Bays and everyone at Elliott and Thompson for seeing something worth printing, and for all the expertise and advice without which this book would still be an unread document on my well-travelled laptop.

Thank you too to all the people who have followed the LSO on tour blog for the last few years. All of you who said that I should write a book ... here it is! Most of all, I want to thank all the members of the mighty London Symphony Orchestra, past and present, without whom none of this would have been possible.

Gareth Davies, March 2013

Index

Page numbers in *italic* refer to illustrations.

About the Author

Gareth Davies is one of the flautists of his generation. Shortly after graduating from the Guildhall School of Music and Drama he was appointed Principal Flute in the Bournemouth Symphony Orchestra at the age of 23. In 2000, Gareth was invited to become Principal Flute with the London Symphony Orchestra where he has remained ever since. During his time there, he has played and recorded with many of the great conductors including Gergiev, Sir Colin Davis, Haitink, Previn, Jansons, Rostropovich and Boulez. A recording of a concerto by Karl Jenkins, written especially for him, is available on EMI, as well as the Nielsen concerto on Naxos. He can be heard on many LSO Live recordings and many film soundtracks including *Star Wars*, *Harry Potter*, *Rise of the Guardians*, *The Queen* and *Brave*.

As well as performing, Gareth is a professor at the Royal College of Music and has given masterclasses in London, New York, Tokyo and Beijing as well as online as part of the YouTube Symphony Orchestra. He is involved in the LSO Discovery programme and recently worked with young people from East London, culminating in a performance at the opening ceremony of the London 2012 Olympic Games. Gareth began writing for the popular LSO On Tour blog and has also written for *Classic FM Magazine* and *BBC Music Magazine*. In addition, he often presents pre-concert talks and has interviewed many conductors and soloists for the orchestra, including Valery Gergiev, Michael Tilson Thomas, Lalo Schifrin, Nikolaj Zneider and Mark Anthony Turnage.

This is his first book.

www.garethdaviesonline.com

London Symphony Orchestra

The London Symphony Orchestra is widely regarded as one of the world's leading orchestras. Since its formation in 1904, it has attracted players from all over the world, many of whom have flourishing solo, chamber music and teaching careers alongside their orchestral work.

The LSO's roster of soloists and conductors includes LSO President Sir Colin Davis, Principal Conductor Valery Gergiev, André Previn as Conductor Laureate, and Daniel Harding and Michael Tilson Thomas as Principal Guest Conductors. Bernard Haitink, Pierre Boulez and Sir Simon Rattle are also regular guests.

The LSO has been Resident Orchestra at the Barbican in the City of London since 1982, presenting over 70 concerts a year to its London audiences, and a further 70 concerts abroad on tour. In addition, the Orchestra has an annual residency at Lincoln Center, New York, and is the international resident orchestra of La Salle Pleyel in Paris, also appearing regularly in Japan and the Far East, as well as in all the major European cities. The LSO is well known for its long association with film music, providing the soundtracks to *Star Wars*, *The King's Speech*, the *Harry Potter* films and many others. The Orchestra also performed at the opening and closing ceremonies of the London 2012 Olympic Games.

Outside the concert hall, the LSO's many other activities include Discovery, the groundbreaking education and community programme, the LSO Live recording label, and the music education centre LSO St Luke's.

www.lso.co.uk

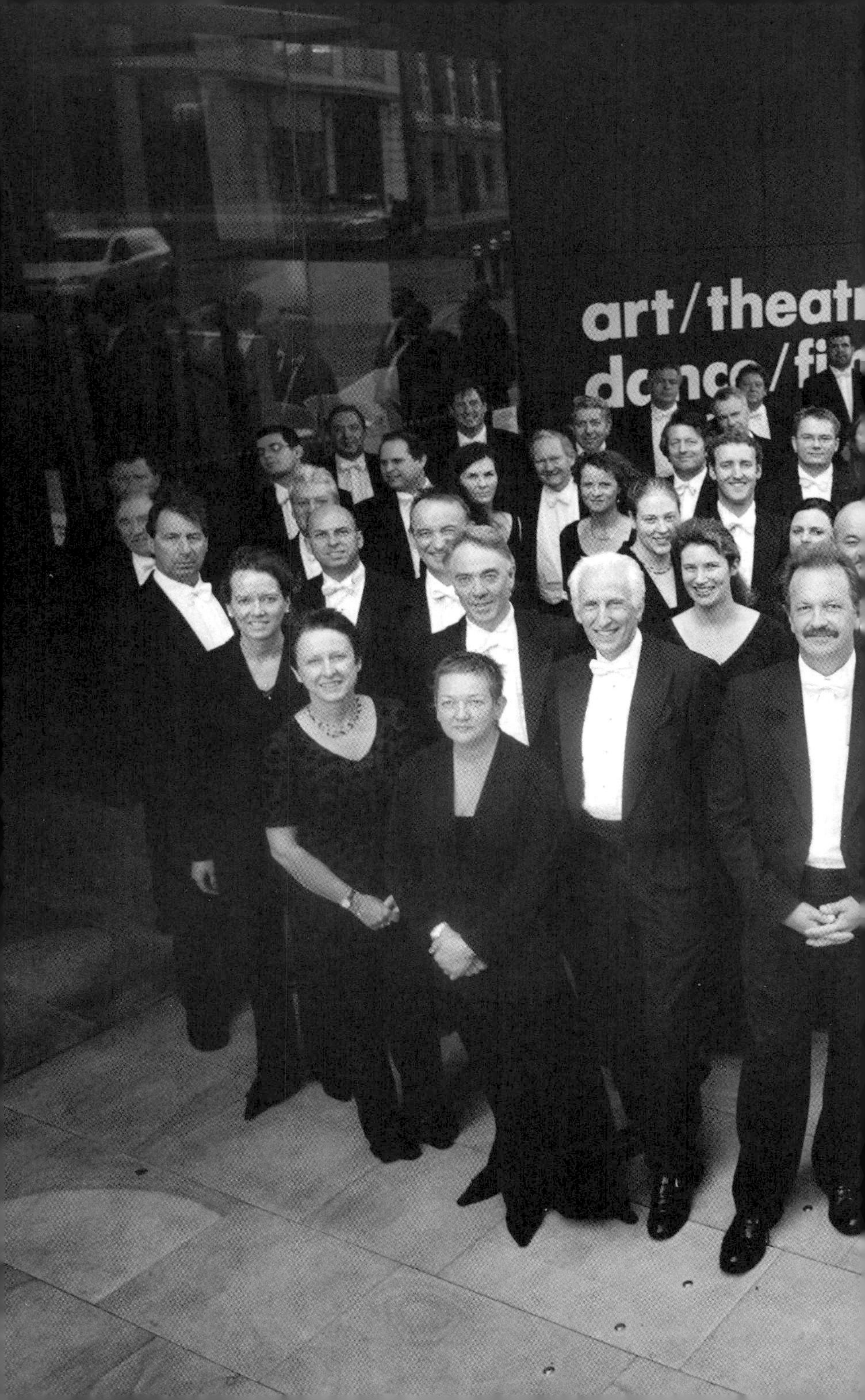
art / theatr